The Mystery and Destiny
of the Church

Sr. Rosena Marie

The Mystery and Destiny of the Church

God's Plan for Our Salvation —
from Eden to the Apocalypse

SOPHIA INSTITUTE PRESS®
Manchester, New Hampshire

Sophia Institute Press®
Box 5284, Manchester, NH 03108
1-800-888-9344
www.sophiainstitute.com

Library of Congress Cataloging-in-Publication Data

Rosena Marie, Sr.
    The mystery and destiny of the church : God's plan for our
salvation – from Eden to the Apocalypse / Rosena Marie.
       p. cm.
    ISBN 978-1-933184-35-7 (pbk. : alk. paper)
    1. Theological anthropology — Christianity.
    2. Salvation — Christianity. 3. Church history. I. Title.
    BT701.3.R67 2008
    262 — dc22
                                2008013972

08 09 10 11 12 9 8 7 6 5 4 3 2 1

To Jesus,
who is our Way,
our Truth, and our Life;
the Alpha and Omega of creation,
to whom be glory and honor
forever and ever. Amen.

Editor's note: The biblical quotations in the following pages are taken from the Douay-Rheims edition of the Old and New Testaments. Where applicable, quotations have been cross-referenced with the differing names and enumeration in the Revised Standard Version, using the following symbol: (RSV =).

Contents

Part 4

The Sixth Day: The Age of the Church

Part 5

The Seventh Day: The Last Things

Introduction

In this time when the echoes of the Great Jubilee proclaimed by our Holy Father Pope John Paul II, to honor the Second Millennium of the birth of Christ, are still lingering with us, it seems appropriate to reflect upon the mystery of the Church that he founded, to bring his salvation to all peoples. This work has been written in an attempt to give a basic idea of what the Church really is, in her nature and destiny, which have unfolded with the passing of the ages.

Since the Church is a work of God, created by his Wisdom and governed by his Providence, it is, like all his works, a profound mystery. It came into being with creation, and was in a state of preparation through all the days of Salvation History until the coming of Christ, who gave it its final form and structure on earth. It will reach its final perfection in heaven. Jesus himself gave the best description of the Church when he said:

> A city seated on a mountain cannot be hid. Neither do men light a candle and put it under a bushel, but upon a candlestick, that it may shine to all that are in the house. Do not think that I have come to destroy the law or the prophets. I have not come to destroy, but to fulfill.[1]

[1] Matt. 5:14-15, 17.

The Mystery and Destiny of the Church

The Church is that city, the City of God on earth, symbolized under the Old Covenant by the holy City of Jerusalem, and under the New Covenant, as the New Jerusalem. St. Paul speaks of heaven, the eternal dwelling place of God, as "that Jerusalem which is above . . . which is our mother."[2] It is described in detail, we might say, in the book of Revelation, chapter 21, and by St. Augustine in his celebrated work *The City of God*. The Church has been compared to many things, which we shall touch upon later in this work; Jesus constantly spoke of it as the kingdom of God on earth.

From the revelation of Christ the Church has also received all that Man can know authentically about God and his works. It is he who supplies the key to the whole mystery of creation and reveals that he himself is the key. It is his presence alone that gives cohesion and meaning to the mystery of the human destiny.

In order, therefore, to grasp the mystery of Christ essentially, we must place him at the heart of creation to see what design or pattern we may discover therein, when examined in the light of his presence. This is what we propose to do, however briefly, in this work, which is a reflection on that spiritual kingdom that he instituted to bring the grace of his redemption to all men.

If this review can help in some way to strengthen the wavering faith of the faithful and deepen their commitment to Jesus and his Church, it will have abundantly fulfilled the purpose for which it has been written.

---

[2] Gal. 4:26.

The Mystery and Destiny
of the Church

Part 1

Man's Eternal Quest

Chapter 1

The Universe as Scripture Reveals It

"In the beginning!" The phrase signifies that awesome moment in eternity — since we can express it in no other way — when God decided to create. He said: "Let it be," and creation came to be. His word of command or his will to create brought it into being. So the phrase "In the beginning" constitutes the great dividing line between time and eternity, for both creation and time began simultaneously.

What lay beyond that dividing line? Nothing but the infinitude of darkness or nonbeing. There is nothing of fable or legend about this statement but, rather, deep and profound theology. The utter absence of being was like a vast and deep sea of darkness. Then, at God's word light was made.[3]

Now there follows an account of the work of the six days of creation, a cosmic account of the universe and all it contains. It treats of the cosmic elements of creation, although not in sequence: light and darkness; the heavens; vegetation, grass, and trees; the sun, the moon, and the stars to govern the light and darkness of day and night, and to govern the seasons and the passage of the years; the creatures to inhabit the waters, from the least to the greatest; the birds of the air; cattle and creeping things of the earth, and beasts of all kinds.

---

[3] Gen. 1:3.

And then God created Man, the last on the list of life but first in dignity and excellence, pinnacle of creation, and highest note in the symphony of life. He made Man in his own image and likeness and appointed him lord of creation, with a mandate to spread over the face of the earth to rule and govern it. With that mandate, the work of creation was complete, and God rested on the seventh day.

When we look at this account of creation, creation of the sun, the moon, and the stars; the fish of the sea and the birds of the air; or the beasts of the field, we find that they are engaging today all the intellectual powers of Man at the highest levels of science and scholarship.

It is the same with chapter 2 of Genesis. The profound mysteries that lie concealed beneath the picturesque description of Eden are foreshadowings of future mysteries of the Church of Christ, and of the entire mystery of redemption. The Tree of Knowledge of Good and Evil is a prophetic foreshadowing of the Fall of Man and the whole tragedy of sin, while the mystic River of Eden foreshadows the grace of redemption encompassing the whole earth, as the following verse expresses it.

> *The mystic River flowing forth*
> *From east to west, to south and north,*
> *Foreshowed redemption's grace divine*
> *Encompassing the earth in time.*[4]

Thus, we may regard these first two chapters of Genesis as the opening chapters of the destiny of the Church on earth.

In the book of Wisdom, the inspired author speaks of the admirable wisdom and providence of God's creative activity, when he says:

---

[4] "Eden" copyright © Sr. Rosena Marie.

Thou hast ordered all things in measure and number and weight. For great power always belonged to thee alone: and who shall resist the strength of thy arm? For the whole world before thee is as the least grain of the balance, and as a drop of the morning dew that falleth upon the earth. But thou hast mercy on all because thou canst do all things, and overlookest the sins of men for the sake of repentance. For thou lovest all things that are, and hatest none of the things which thou hast made; for thou didst not appoint or make anything, hating it. And how could anything endure if thou wouldst not, or be preserved if not called by thee? But thou sparest all because they are thine, O Lord who lovest souls.[5]

As we have said, when God uttered his Fiat, both creation and time began, and with them began also the mystery of the Church. For the Church is the household of God on earth, a pattern of the Divine Household of heaven. It pervades the whole of creation with whose destiny it is inextricably involved.[6] And as the Church began at the moment of creation, its destiny began to evolve through time, and will continue to do so until the end of the world. The record of its destiny in time is the history of the Church on earth, which we call Salvation History. The record of its destiny began when God placed Man on trial as a first test of his fidelity, which is recounted in chapter 3 of the book of Genesis, and from that moment, it continued to evolve throughout the ages.

When we look at the scriptural record, it seems at first glance to be no more than a simple account of separate events in the history of mankind, but when we look back over the whole, it is seen

[5] Wisd. 11:21-27.
[6] Cf. Rom. 8:22.

to have a marvelous cohesion and design. Everything is in fact interrelated, and all is directed by God to a determined goal; that goal is Christ. By the preordained will of the eternal Father, it was Christ who gave the Church its final form and aspect. We know this from Jesus' own testimony when he laid his credentials before the world during his public life.

Born in Bethlehem about the year 6 BC, as far as modern scholarship can determine, he spent about thirty years of his life in his hometown of Nazareth. This period is usually called the hidden life. At the end of that time, John the Baptist came forth from his solitude in the desert in which he had lived for about twenty years, to call the nation to prayer and penance, because the Messiah was at hand. At that hour, Jesus left his home village of Nazareth forever and began the period of his public life, which lasted about two years and a few months. His public life ended with his Passion and death on Calvary. It was during his public life that he declared himself to be the Messiah — that is, the Savior promised by God in Eden. And it was during this period also that he founded his Church to bring the grace of his salvation to all men.

In the light of these facts, it is interesting to recall what he said of his own identity and mission both to his adversaries and to his friends. To the scribes and Pharisees and the religious authorities in Jerusalem who had refused to accept him or his claims, he said:

> Search the Scriptures: for you think in them to have life everlasting. And the same are they that give testimony of me. And you will not come to me that you may have life. I am come in the name of my Father, and you receive me not: if another shall come in his own name, him you will receive. How can you believe, who receive glory one from

another and the glory which is from God alone you do not seek? Think not that I will accuse you to the Father. There is one that accuses you: Moses, in whom you trust. For if you did believe Moses, you would perhaps believe me also: for he wrote of me. But if you do not believe his writings, how will you believe my words?[7]

And on the day of his Resurrection, he rebuked the two disciples of Emmaus because they refused to believe the testimony of the holy women who said that he was risen from the dead. He said to them: " 'O foolish and slow of heart to believe in all things which the prophets have spoken. Ought not Christ to have suffered these things and so to enter into his glory?' And beginning at Moses and all the prophets, he expounded to them in all the Scriptures the things that were concerning him."

All the while that he had been walking with them, they did not recognize him. It was only during the supper they invited him to share that they recognized him in the breaking of bread, and when he had vanished from their sight, they said to each other: "Was not our heart burning within us while he spoke in the way and opened to us the Scriptures?"[8]

And on the same evening, after he had taken supper with his disciples to convince them of the reality of his Resurrection, he said to them concerning all that he had previously foretold them about his Passion, death and Resurrection: "These are the words which I spoke to you while I was yet with you, that all things must needs be fulfilled which are written in the law of Moses and in prophets and in the psalms, concerning me." Then he opened

---

[7] John 5:39-47.
[8] Luke 24:25-27, 32.

their understanding, that they might understand the Scriptures. And he said to them:

> "Thus it is written, and thus it behoved Christ to suffer and to rise again from the dead, the third day: and that penance and remission of sins should be preached in his name, unto all nations, beginning at Jerusalem. And you are witnesses of these things. And I send the promise of my Father upon you: but stay in the city till you be endued with power from on high."
>
> And he led them out as far as Bethania, and lifting up his hands he blessed them. And it came to pass, while he blessed them, he departed from them and was carried up to heaven. And they adoring went back into Jerusalem with great joy.[9]

With this divine blessing, the Church of Christ, upon which the Holy Spirit would soon descend, at Pentecost, was ready to set out on her journey through time. And we, secure in the reliability of these awesome revelations and events, from the mouth of Truth itself can now stand by the wayside of time to watch her pilgrimage through the ages on her way to her eternal homeland.

[9] Luke 24:44-52.

Chapter 2

The Universe as It Reveals Itself

Because Man is a rational being, he is perpetually occupied with the why of everything he sees. Unlike the animal, whose mental activity stops at the object it perceives, Man goes beyond the object to find its hidden source. In nothing is this intellectual activity more evident than in his ceaseless preoccupation with the universe of which he forms a part. He looks upon this visible creation and is filled with wonder at the order and harmony that pervade it. It is a silent question mark provoking him to reflection, an orb of splendor hung in the halls of space, which in every age has captivated him by its beauty and engaged all his powers of intellect by its mystery. What is it? Where did it come from, and why has it come to be?

His thought as he beholds it could best be expressed, perhaps, in the words of a psalm: "O Lord our God, how admirable is your name in all the earth! When I consider the heavens, the work of your hands, the moon and the stars which you have set."[10]

Totally unlike the angelic creation, which is spiritual and invisible, the universe is purely material in its composition, yet it glorifies God most wonderfully by its order, harmony, and beauty and serves him in its own appointed way by its unfailing obedience to law. But although it is purely material in its composition, it is

[10] Cf. Ps. 8:2, 4 (RSV = Ps. 8:1, 3).

nonetheless mysterious, for its basic element, which is matter, is undefinable, as one author so well expressed it:

> We can say a great deal about matter, about its laws of change and movement, its mass, charges, and valences, its molecules, atoms, and electrons. We can say a great deal about the physical, chemical, and biological properties of matter, but we cannot define matter. We cannot define just what belongs to its essence.[11]

So here, at the very outset, we are confronted with baffling mystery. What shall we say, then, when we begin to investigate further this mysterious orb whose basic fabric eludes the most searching scrutiny of Man?

Expanding simultaneously in all directions from just one central point, the universe appears as an ever-growing sphere, and each of its material parts is a sphere. The marvels that it reveals in its composition and governing laws are so mysterious and profound that it overwhelms the imagination. In its internal constitution, the universe reflects the pattern of human society itself, for as no single individual in society exists unto himself, so no single star in the universe exists independently, but belongs to a specific star group. The smallest star group in the universe is a solar system like the one to which our earth belongs. It is the family unit of the universe, so to speak, the sun like the father of the family, dominating the entire group of planets that revolve around it in concentric circles, thus preserving the order and balance of the entire system.

In our solar system, for example, the planets are held in perfect position by a power of attraction in the sun, which draws them to

---

[11] Cf. E. J. Fortman, *Everlasting Life After Death* (New York: Alba House, 1976), 244.

itself, and a power of counterattraction in the planets, which enables them to resist this attraction. This dual law of attraction and counterattraction is operative throughout the entire universe and preserves the balance and harmony of the whole. But like the human family itself, the solar system is a unit of a much larger group that we call a galaxy; we could say that the galaxies are "the states" of the "Star Nation," which is the universe. Modern science has discovered that there are about a hundred billion galaxies in the universe — one million alone being discernible in the bowl of the Great Dipper, from the observatory on Mount Polomar.[12] (We might observe here that all of these figures relating to distances and related matters of astronomy are constantly liable to change as science makes new discoveries.)

The galaxies stretch far away into the unchartered regions of outer space, each revolving upon itself as it plunges with incredible speed through these infinite regions of darkness, and all the while, each star within each galaxy is likewise revolving upon itself; yet all the stars within the galaxy remain in perfect position, relative to one another, while the galaxies themselves do likewise. The effect of this principle of motion that is operative throughout the universe is similar to that which occurs when a balloon is inflated with air. Thus, the universe is like a vast balloon that is constantly expanding, while preserving its symmetry unchanged.

The galaxies lie at immense distances from one another, being sometimes separated by a distance of billions of light-years. In outer space, distances are so great that scientists reckon them in terms of time rather than in terms of miles. So a light-year is the number of miles that light travels in one year. Since light travels

---

[12] Cf. Kenneth Weaver and James P. Blair, "The Incredible Universe," *National Geographic* CXLV-V (May 1974): 592.

at the rate of 186,282 miles per second, this would be 6 quadrillion (6,000,000,000,000) miles per year. The farthest object discernible through the 200-inch telescope on Mount Polomar is about 10 billion light-years away from us. This represents the limits of the known universe at present, but we can reasonably surmise that these exceedingly remote galaxies are merely springboards to still more remote worlds of the Star Nation.

The galaxy to which our solar system belongs contains a hundred billion stars and is shaped somewhat like a wheel. Our sun is situated about 30 million light-years from its central point, while the farthest stars in the galaxy are about 80 million light-years away from us. It takes our sun about two billion years to travel around the galaxy. The nearest star in our galaxy to our sun is four and a half light-years away from us; it is called Alpha Centauri. The only galaxy we can see with unaided vision is almost two million light-years away.

Of particular interest to us is that part of the universe which is our home. The earth is a unit of the solar system that comprises the sun and nine planets that revolve around it in concentric circles. The sun, which is the head and center of the system, is a star of medium size and middle age, and is one million times larger than the earth. Counting outward from the sun, the planets that revolve around it are Mercury, Venus, Earth, Mars, Jupiter, Saturn, Uranus, Neptune, and Pluto. The earth revolves on its own axis at the rate of over a thousand miles per hour as it traces a path around the sun. Its rotation upon itself causes night and day, while its rotation around the sun determines the seasons of the year.

But there is one element on this planet that makes it unique among all the galaxies of the universe: this is the mysterious thing we call life, which forms an element of this material creation. When the earth was ready to receive it, God placed upon it a hierarchy of life that bears upon itself the impress of beauty and design which are characteristic of all the works of God. When Man turns his attention to this hierarchy, he quickly perceives that he has come face-to-face with one of the most mysterious chapters in the book of creation, for he finds himself in the presence of a fathomless ocean of mystery. To begin with, the laws by which it is governed are so mysterious that they resist in large measure his every effort to penetrate them.

This hierarchy comprises three distinct kingdoms, each subject to its own specific laws, yet they abide in harmony with one another and are in many ways dependent upon one another for their common well-being. The principle of life as it manifests itself in each of these various kingdoms, whether plant, animal, or human, is most wonderful and mysterious. It exists in beings so small that they seem to stand on the periphery of nothingness, and ascends in order of excellence through the plant and animal kingdoms until it reaches the highly complex principle of life that is found in Man.

In the vegetable kingdom, for example, the recurring cycle of the seasons, with their exquisite pattern of beauty and color, is a source of never-ending delight, yet this unending cycle of change is always the same: paradoxically we might call it the changeless cycle of change.

In the animal kingdom, likewise, the principle of life is most mysterious in its manifestations, for it implies much more than the power of self-movement; it involves that marvelous power we call instinct, by which a bird, for example, knows how to procure the proper food to sustain itself, guide its own flight hither and thither, migrate to a warmer climate in winter and return again in summer, and seeks to preserve itself in being until the end of time.

Chapter 3

The Nature of Man

The perfection with which everything in nature obeys its appointed laws leaves Man breathless with admiration, for he sees at a glance that this unfailing obedience is the source of the marvelous order and harmony that pervade the universe. But he also perceives that this obedience is rendered of necessity and not of free choice. Moreover, the whole creation, whether animate or inanimate, is unaware of the obedience it renders to law, unaware indeed of its own existence.

Besides, the activities of the animal kingdom reveal a static perfection, which knows neither ascent to a higher, nor descent to a lower level of efficiency. We may marvel at the perfection with which the bird builds its nest, or the bee its hive, but we know that this efficiency is governed by a fixed norm of perfection. Ten thousand years ago, the bird built its nest exactly as it does today, and ten thousand years from now, it will still build it in exactly the same way.

In the case of Man, it is vastly different, for he alone of all created beings can act of his own free will, and this brings up the question of his presence and status in the universe. Reflecting upon his own nature, he perceives how greatly he differs from the other kingdoms of life that surround him. Indeed, as the ancient philosophers held, he is a microcosm of the universe himself and far more complex than the universe of which he finds himself a part. He owns kinship with every type of being that surrounds him, yet, while resembling all, he immeasurably surpasses all. With the inanimate creation, for example, he shares the elements of his physical nature; with the plant kingdom he shares his vegetative nature; with the animal kingdom, his sense nature; but in the possession of a rational nature, he surpasses them all. It is this which gives him a new dimension of being, so to speak, and makes him lord of the universe.

His soul makes him a point of contact between the world of matter and the world of spirit. In comparison with the universe, he is only as a grain of sand, but in the possession of a rational soul, he becomes its moral center and its lord. By his powers of intellect, he is not only aware of his own existence and that of the material creation, but he can hold the entire universe within the confines of his own mind, so to speak. In the light of his intellect, he can estimate its every dimension, analyze its every element, and channel its vast powers to serve his every need. Moreover, he can mentally encompass the mystery of time, making the past become present through the faculty of memory, and making the future become present through the faculty of imagination. The eye of his intellect is not circumscribed by the horizons of time or space.

Again, by his powers of intellect, he can translate the concepts of his mind into the external realities of language, music, painting, sculpture, and architecture and furnish tools and implements of all kinds for his own use. And all of these things he has done from the beginning, for from the very dawn of human history, all the artifacts that can be proved to be of human origin give evidence of Man's intellectual activity.

Thus, from the beginning, Man fashioned tools for his own use, according to his own specifications, something that no animal can ever do. Beginning with tools of unpolished stone, he quickly discarded them for tools of polished stone, and thence, by a swift upward flight, he passed from tools of stone to artifacts of bronze and iron until he has now reached the conquests of the space age.

Even when he dwelt in caves, he did not dwell there as an animal in its den but as a proprietor in a home, for he adorned his cave with beautiful drawings and paintings. Modern science has discovered many fine specimens of prehistoric art dating from the early stone age onward; these include objects in bone, bronze, iron, and wood, and exhibit both fine workmanship and fine art. As time went on, he developed the basic skills and crafts of domestic life as he discovered the need and benefit to be derived from them. Thus, he began the widespread domestication of animals about 14,000 years ago, and the controlled raising of crops and agriculture as well as the domestic arts of spinning and weaving about 10,000 years ago.

This is Man as he sees himself in the scale of created being, the highest note in the Symphony of Life within this visible universe.

Confronted with this ocean of natural mystery in which he finds himself immersed, he is compelled by his rational nature to ask: What is it? Where did it come from? And why has it come to be?

It would be an affront to his intelligence to say that it all just happened by chance, for no thinking mind could content itself with such an uncritical conclusion. To begin with, every effect must have a cause, and the universe is no exception. Moreover, since being of itself cannot evolve from sheer nothingness, it follows that the universe of itself could not have come to be. Again, the order and harmony that are everywhere evident in creation rule out the possibility of chance, since it is a matter of universal experience that order does not of itself evolve from chaos: it is always the result of design.

As a rational being, therefore, Man is compelled to find a reasonable explanation of the universe, for everything in it shows it to be the work of an intelligent author, who must be the principle or first cause of its being. Thus, in effect, he is led by his reason to acknowledge the existence of God. God is not an invention of Man's imagination, and if Man wishes to obtain an authentic answer to the reason of being of the universe and to the mystery of his own presence and status within it, it is from God alone that he can hope to receive it. Human science can presume, in some measure at least, to answer the *how* of the universe but it can never answer the *why*. God alone can do that.

Part 2

What Is Man?

Chapter 4

The Body of Man

Man has been from the beginning much preoccupied with the mystery of his own presence and status in creation. His reflections upon his own nature and destiny could well be summed up in the words of the inspired psalmist:

> What is Man that you are mindful of him, or the son of Man that you care for him? You have made him a little less than the angels, you have crowned him with glory and honor and set him over the works of your hands. You have subjected all things under his feet, all sheep and cattle together with all the beasts of the field, the birds of the air and the fishes of the sea, that pass through the paths of the sea. O Lord our God, how admirable is your name in all the earth."[13]

It is not known exactly how long Man has been on the earth. For the last century or two, it seemed fairly certain that his presence here was to be reckoned not in thousands but possibly in hundreds of thousands of years; but as science began to discover more and more significant facts about the presence of life in general on earth, scientists began to move the first appearance of Man farther and farther back in time. One fact we know for certain is that Man was the last to make his appearance on the list of life. In this, the

---

[13] Ps. 8:5-10 (RSV = Ps. 8:4-9).

teaching of divine revelation and the findings of science concur. This is a highly important fact, because Man's appearance on earth stands in proportion to the appearance of life in general.

The most recent scientific discoveries assert that the first appearance of life on earth occurred very soon after our planet became solid rock. This occurred about five billion years ago, and life is believed to have first appeared about three and a half billion years ago. It follows, therefore, that since Man is the last on the list of life, his appearance cannot have been too far behind, perhaps a billion or two billion years ago. It is awesome to think upon this possibility, yet when we consider that the universe is about 13 billion years old, our galaxy 10 billion, and our earth about 5 billion, Man's sojourn here is as brief as a day. To the unbeliever, he is no more than the perfection of animal life, a creature whose existence is circumscribed by the limits of space and time, destined to flourish for a day like the flower of the field and then to fade like the little field flower into the oblivion of nothingness.

Yet it must be admitted, even by those who hold such opinions, that there is something in Man that sets him apart from all other types of life that surround him. It may be difficult to explain, but it is evident to all. What constitutes this radical difference is, in reality, the presence of a rational soul, which manifests itself in the intellectual activity of which Man alone is capable.

The Church defines Man as a creature composed of body and soul and made in the image and likeness of God. It is this union of body and soul that makes the individual person. A body without a soul is not a man but a corpse, just as a soul without a body is not a man but a disembodied spirit. Man, therefore, is neither a purely material nor a purely spiritual creature; he is, rather, a union of matter and spirit. Any consideration of the nature of Man, therefore, must take these two constituent elements into account.

Let us begin, then, with a brief consideration of the material element in Man, his body. The first question science asks when investigating the origin of Man is: *Where did he come from, or how did he first come to be?* It cannot presume as yet to answer that question definitively; the most it can do is to formulate theories, which, in the last analysis, mean conjecture. As in the case of the other types of life on the earth, the most widely discussed theory to explain the origin and development of human life is that of evolution, for this theory involves the question of Man no less than the other sectors of the animate creation. Unfortunately, however, it is one of the most misunderstood theories of today.

It is well to remember here again that the theory of evolution in regard to the origin of Man, like that of life in general, is only a theory, not a fact. Much confusion can arise when matters that are only theories are proclaimed as facts. It is also well to remember that no theory can ever become a fact or be more worthy of belief simply because it is accepted by the majority, for any theory is always and only a conjecture. In matters of this kind, to offer a contrary opinion to that accepted by the majority is to expose ourselves to ridicule as being old-fashioned, out of step with the times, or unwilling to face facts.

To return now to the question of Man's origins, there are those who hold that the human body was evolved from the ape or some lower animal form; whether it actually was or was not is still an open question, despite the pictorial drawings of charts in museums or books, or the carefully built-up hypotheses that are so common today, for as we have said, all of this is pure speculation. Indeed, it is extremely difficult for any proponent of evolution to make a single factual statement about the origin of the first human body.

What does the Church say about this matter? She says, in effect, that the human body could have been produced in either of two ways: first, immediately, by a direct act of God's creative power, without any intervening agency or cause in its construction; or secondly, it could have been formed mediately by God — that is, although created by God, his body developed through evolution.

St. Thomas Aquinas held to the first opinion, that of direct creation, although admitting the possibility of the second. St. Augustine held to the second, that of mediate creation by God. Both were men of great intellectual genius, and both were great saints. We see from this that the Church is not opposed to the theory of evolution in itself as a possible explanation of the origin of Man's body, for this does not contradict the concepts or teachings of divine revelation.

But she rejects emphatically any theory which asserts that the evolution of the human body from a subhuman or nonhuman species, if it ever occurred, happened as a result of some blind evolutionary process; rather, she inviolably holds and teaches that God is the necessary cause and first principle of Man, as he is of all being and life. If the body of Man evolved from some lower animal form, it was not produced by the unaided natural powers of a lower parentage but by the determinate will and purpose of the Creator, and subject to his guiding providence. To maintain the idea of a blind evolution in regard to the origin of the human body would be contrary to both divine revelation and right reason.

In regard to the Church's opinion on the idea of Man's mediate creation, that is, his bodily origin by means of evolution, she says that mediate formation of the human body, if God actually chose that method, could extend over an unknown period of time. It could take place also through a preparation that would entail a progressive growth from the lower forms of life. This would be done by means of "special powers" instilled by God; for instance, the functioning and development of an animal body would be directed toward reaching a stage wherein, materially, it would be ready to be made human and to become the body of the first man. The human body would have been produced in the original creation in a virtual or latent way. Its actual production would still be God's work, taking place according to his guidance, and according to his plan; but it would be a mediate production, coming upon the face of the earth after passing through many developing processes.

Has contemporary science succeeded in discovering traces of such processes? Those who uphold the theory of evolution will reply in the affirmative, and some of them will even venture to expound and correlate the earlier progressive steps of the supposed evolutionary process with astounding precision. We have only to think of the drawings in magazines or the hypothetical skeletal constructions in museums to be convinced of this. Yet the actual evidence brought forward thus far, after careful analysis, proves insufficient to warrant the publicizing of these expositions and correlations as the true story of what actually happened. There seems to be too much guesswork involved in them. However, the traces discovered by the natural sciences have established the theory of evolution as tenable, as a working hypothesis at least, and it would be unreasonable to deny this fact.

It must be admitted, however, in any impartial consideration of the question that there are valid arguments on both sides. On the one hand, there are many points that could be invoked to uphold the theory of evolution, but on the other hand, there is much evidence rooted in nature itself that would seem to indicate that Man was never anything else but Man.

Take, for example, the physical appearance of Man. There is no one who will deny that even in his physical appearance Man excels the brute creation, for God intended the body of Man to enshrine a spiritual soul. By its powers to feel and perceive, it was destined to provide impressions that the soul could purify into thought. Thus it was intended to be an instrument for intellectual operation. The position of its parts, moreover, their functioning and alignment, their interrelation and all the workings of the human organism furnish incontrovertible testimony to the singular and noble destiny God willed for Man. His body is a triumph of design.

The defects of Man's bodily constitution are only those defects that are inherent in all matter. They are defects that, by the very nature of things, have to be in the makeup of a being who is essentially composed of material elements, as Man is. It was necessary to God's design for Man that he be composed both of matter and spirit, since he was destined to be a connecting link between the material and spiritual worlds. Indeed, these apparent defects are really not defects at all; they appear as such only when an improper comparison is made between matter and spirit.

It may be maintained, however, that by comparison with the lower animals, Man's physical nature shows defect, for his senses are in some instances less keen than theirs: his vision, for example, is not as keen as the eagle's nor his hearing as acute as the dog's. But again, we must assert that this apparent deficiency is no real defect when considered in the light of the purpose that lies behind the senses of Man.

All the sense powers of his body were designed to serve the higher faculty of reason, and thus, a certain balance and moderation were necessary in view of this ulterior work assigned them. If his senses were overly sharp, they would prove a hindrance rather than a help; as it is, however, he is seldom troubled by an overly acute sense of sight or hearing.

Moreover, by his intellectual genius, Man can supplement his own sense faculties in a way that is altogether beyond the powers of the animal. Thus, by means of binoculars, telescopes, sound detectors, and a multitude of other highly sophisticated scientific instruments, he can magnify his sense of vision so that he can clearly behold objects located at a distance of billions of light years away or receive faint sounds from the stars and galaxies in far distant regions of the universe. Then again, in his sense of touch, Man naturally excels all other sentient beings; he likewise takes precedence in the quality of his interior senses because his imagination and memory far surpass anything the animals possess.

Coming now to the question of Man's physical appearance, what is immediately striking is the absence of those characteristics that would place him in the category of a mere brute beast. Indeed, to those who uphold the "survival of the fittest" theory of evolution, this must present a singularly difficult problem. For those who say that Man was originally a species of brute who struggled up from some dark depth to his present lordly status in the animal kingdom, the complete absence of any type of natural equipment with which to wage such a struggle for survival is singularly striking.

Of all the animals, Man is the most ill-fitted to carry on the vicious war for existence that the proponents of this theory assert as a matter of fact. He has neither horns, tusks, claws, nor hide — nothing in fact that could ensure his survival if he were a mere brute animal. In the design of God, it was specifically intended to be just that way, for Man is not purely an animal: he is, rather, a rational animal, and his gift of reason more than compensates for the lack of natural equipment so necessary to the brute beast for its protection and survival.

By his intellectual genius, he can manufacture weapons for his self-defense and clothing and shelter for his own needs. The number and variety of artifacts he can thus produce are innumerable, while the various ways by which his reason enables him to adapt himself to varying conditions of climate or geographical location, for example, are unexplainable, except on the premises that Man is not a brute animal but rather a rational animal — that is, a human being.

From these considerations, we can see that it is necessary to proceed with caution in any evaluation of the origin of Man. We cannot accept the animal origin of Man as an established fact, even though it be widely proclaimed or accepted as such. It is a difficult and complex problem that only time will perhaps resolve. Evolution might have occurred; if this is ever definitively proved, it will be a further example of the marvelous works of God.

The theory of evolution was unknown to the Hebrews and the animals are represented as created according to "their kinds" or their species, such as they were known to have been at the time Genesis was written. What the book offers is a popular account, suited to the mentality of the age, and directed to a purely religious purpose. It was not the wish of the Holy Spirit, in inspiring the sacred writers, to teach men about evolution or such matters of purely secular knowledge. Thus, if it should ever be established that the human body evolved from lower forms, the religious teaching of Genesis would remain the same — namely, that the world was created for the sake of Man, who is himself the work of God's hands, no matter what path the Divine Wisdom chose to follow in the production of Man's bodily frame.

That Man has a spiritual rational soul is established by philosophy, as is also the fact that such a spiritual substance could not have its origin in anything material. And it is due to Man's spiritual soul that his mental powers differ essentially from those of even the highest of the brute creation. The refined concept of spiritual being, however, was not attained until many centuries after the time of Moses.

Pope Pius XII reminded us in his encyclical *Humani generis* that the question does not belong exclusively to the field of natural science and that the sources of revelation impose caution and moderation. It is one that may be freely discussed, provided we are prepared to accept the decision of the Church, to whom Christ committed the charge of interpreting Holy Scripture and of guarding the doctrines of the Faith.

In the same encyclical, Pope Pius XII said that, as regards polygenism, Catholics do not enjoy the same liberty. For the faithful cannot embrace the opinion that after Adam there lived on this earth true men not derived from him by natural generation, or that Adam signifies a plurality of first parents.

But all of our considerations thus far have been concerned mainly with the physical element in Man — namely, his body — yet we know that beyond this material element, there is a whole world in Man, which it is beyond the competence of natural science to investigate; this other element is his soul, upon which we shall now reflect in order to complete our study of Man in the totality of his being.

Chapter 5

The Soul of Man

Both divine revelation and philosophy have established that Man
has a spiritual, rational soul. The Church defines the soul of Man
as a spirit possessing understanding and free will and made in the
likeness of God. It is not a pure spirit, since it is united to the material element of Man's nature, yet it belongs to the glorious hierarchy of spiritual being, although occupying the lowest place
therein. The angels, whether good or bad, are superior in nature to
the soul of Man, since they are pure spirits having no material element in their composition. At the summit of the hierarchy of spiritual being stands God, supreme and infinite, the Being of beings,
to whom everything that exists owes its being.[14] Nevertheless, the
soul, although the lowest in this hierarchy of matterless being, is
like both to the angels and to God himself, in that it possesses understanding and free will.

Speaking of the nature of the soul, the Church further says that
it is simple. In the philosophic sense, this means that it is not made
up of component parts, as a material object would be. Since the
soul has no matter in its composition, it cannot have separate
parts. We could express this in another way by saying that once
the soul has come to be, it is a perfect human soul in the first
moment of its existence; that means that it is a substantial being,

---

[14] John 1:1-3; Acts 17:28.

existing in and by itself, needing no other substance in which to maintain itself. It does not undergo any kind of progressive development, nor is it the product of successive adaptations. It does not attain to its perfection through growth; rather, if we might express it thus, it has all of its being always.

Because it is a spirit, the soul is invisible, but its existence is known from its acts: the acts proper to the soul are to reason, to think, and to will. These acts are high above the power of flesh and blood. The human mind is able to reflect upon itself; it is able to understand that it is understanding, and this is something the animal can never do.

By its nature, the intellect moves in the realm of the abstract; it deals with concepts and ideas and with universal principles, as contrasted with the senses, which are preoccupied with particulars alone. It penetrates to the essence that lies hidden behind the visible reality. We could express it in another way by saying that the intellect discovers the realm of the intelligible, hidden away in the sensible, and finds the immutable nature of reality clothed in the mutable things of sense. In a word, it apprehends the meaning of things that are buried beneath the changeableness of the world of sensible phenomena.

Besides its faculty of reason, the soul also possesses the faculty of memory, which is far superior to that of the animal, and likewise the faculty of the will, which is altogether absent in the animal kingdoms of life. Man alone possesses the ability to distinguish and freely choose between alternatives of good and evil. These vast powers are completely beyond the range of the animal's powers of sense perception.

In view of its nature, the Church holds and teaches that each human soul is created directly by God, called forth from nothingness by a direct act of his divine creative power. It is not evolved from anyone or anything; indeed, it could not exist at all except by a special act of creation, given the nature of its being.

Of particular interest to Man in every age is the question of the soul's ultimate destiny. Is it extinguished with the death of his body, or does it continue to live on thereafter? On this question there are basically two schools of thought. The first says that when the body of Man dissolves into dust after death, his soul disappears with it. This is the theory of the materialists who say that Man is purely material in his nature — that is, that he has no purely spiritual principle of life in the composition of his being. According to this theory, everything that Man does can be explained as a kind of chemical process: Man is simply a refined type of machine, and his powers of thought, his wisdom and science and the whole world of his ideas are merely the linking together of sensations and sense images. His mind and consciousness and all his intellectual achievements are merely the products of a general evolution that has been going on in the universe since the beginning of time.

It follows as a logical consequence of this theory, that all of Man's intellectual powers and activities are destined to ultimate dissolution and destruction, since they are material in their very essence and therefore subject to the same laws of disintegration as those which govern all material things.

Opposed to this idea of the death of the soul is the school of thought that says the soul indeed survives after the death of the body, but the advocates of this opinion are not agreed upon what kind of survival it is. Some hold, for example, that it is swallowed up in something greater than itself and thus loses its identity in some vague and indefinable absolute. This line of thought is a feature of Hindu philosophy and of Buddhism.

The Church rejects both of these theories — namely, that Man is merely and solely a material being whose soul dies with his body, or, on the other hand, that the soul survives after death but loses its identity in some vague absolute. To all such erroneous concepts she opposes the certain teaching of divine revelation. She says that the soul of Man is incapable of destruction. Since it is an individual spirit when united to the body on earth, it will continue to be an individual spirit after its separation from the body in death. It cannot die because it is a spirit and therefore of its very nature has no component parts: since, as we have said, death is a dissolution into component parts, it is impossible for the soul to die. Moreover, the very idea of absorption in the bosom of the absolute is abhorrent to its being. The complete teaching of the Church regarding the soul of Man could be summed up by saying that each individual human soul is directly created by God and is immortal.

It takes the union of body and soul to make the person, and it is the Creator who effects this union. And when, for the first time, God infused a spiritual, rational soul into a material body, the first Man was created. If, as we have already said, God created Man directly, then he himself prepared the first human body to enshrine the first human soul; if, on the other hand, he created Man mediately — that is, indirectly, by allowing the body of Man to evolve from some lower animal form — then we may presume that he infused a rational soul into the animal body only after it had been sufficiently developed and ennobled in form and aspect to receive it. Divine revelation calls the first Man *Adam*, which means "the Man." By whichever method God chose to create the first Man, we know that he, Adam, was the father of the human race.

Because he is composed of body and soul, Man stands as a point of contact between two worlds: the world of matter and the world of spirit. In the possession of a body, he is akin to the animal, but in the possession of a soul, he is akin to the angel. Yet although he resembles the animal in the physical aspect of his nature, he is not purely material, and although he resembles the angel in the possession of a soul, he is not purely spiritual; rather, he is placed between the angel and the animal, sharing something of the nature and destiny of both. His body is subject to the law of disintegration, but his soul is created to live forever.

Man stands at the pinnacle of creation, its crowning glory and its lord. Indeed, precisely because he possesses a rational soul, he is the moral center of the universe. His presence therein changes it from being a mere place into a home, of which he is the sole proprietor under God.

This is Man, the most excellent note, as we have said, in the great symphony of life in this visible creation. Let us now turn to consider what the Church tells us from divine revelation about this masterpiece of God's creative power.

Chapter 6

The First Man

In view of what modern science has found regarding the great
length of Man's sojourn on earth, since his first appearance at the
end of the third or the beginning of the fourth geological period,
what is to be said about the account of his origin as set forth in the
first three chapters of Genesis? In other words, is the story of Eden
actually true? Did it really happen, or can the scientific theories
about the possible origin of Man be reconciled with what divine
revelation teaches in the book of Genesis, or are both accounts in-
compatible or even contradictory?

Fortunately, they can both be held and both be reconciled, but
before proceeding further, it is well to recall what we said in a previous chapter about the relationship in which divine revelation
and science stand one to the other. They are like two circles revolving on the same axis, although moving on different planes
around the mystery of God. Science moves on a natural or lower
plane, while divine revelation moves on a supernatural or higher
plane. Science concerns itself with the *how* and *when* of created
things. Divine revelation concerns itself with the *who* and *why* of
created things. It is in the light of these facts that we must examine the story of Eden as it is recounted in Genesis. As we have
already said, these chapters in Genesis are neither a scientific
statement nor a formal history as we know history today, and it was
never intended to be such. They are therefore outside the sphere

of scientific investigation altogether; it is theology that should concern itself with them and judge them in the light of divine revelation.

So, did the story of Eden actually happen in real life? We can only reply that we do not know, and perhaps we shall never know. It would be futile to speculate whether the author of Genesis is recounting actual fact or employing a literary symbol, in the story of our first parents in Eden. That it could have actually happened in that way is certainly within the realm of possibility, for as the old proverb says, "There are facts that are stranger than fiction." Then, as regards the actual facts of the narration, God could have made known these things to the inspired author of Genesis by means of a revelation.

We have only to think, for example, of how he has often made known the most secret sins of total strangers to the saints in every age, things that, in a natural sense, they could never have known, and this, not to embarrass the poor person concerned but to help and heal him. The holy Curé of Ars and St. John Bosco offer examples of such revelations made by God in our own day, and most of all, the world-renowned Padre Pio, who was famous for his knowledge of the most hidden secrets of men's hearts. In regard to the scriptural account of the book of Genesis of the creation of Man, we do not know whether the inspired author received such a direct revelation from God, since there is no explicit mention of such.

How, then, does the Church look upon the account of Man's origin in these first three chapters of Genesis? She holds and teaches that these chapters are all divinely inspired.

Whether they are narrating actual fact or are merely employed by the inspired author as a literary symbol, they contain a very important theological statement about the nature and destiny of

Man. This theological truth is the inspired thought of the scriptural account.

It is really unimportant, therefore, in the last analysis, whether the story of Eden is actual fact or literary symbol, for whichever way it is, the theological truths about Man that the story contains are what is ultimately important. These theological statements are always true, regardless of what science may discover, and it is these we shall now consider as they are explained by the Church, the fruit of her deep reflection, guided by the Holy Spirit, upon this inspired account of Man's origin and destiny.

The first fact this divinely inspired account of Man's origin gives is that he was created by God; whatever the manner of his creation, God is the Author of his being, as he is of all being and life. Furthermore, from the very beginning, God intended Man to have a special destiny, vastly different from that of the other kingdoms of life that surrounded him. This is signified by the fact that the scriptural account represents God as taking counsel with himself before creating Man. It was a figurative way of saying that, in the infinite plenitude of his Being, he willed to crown his creation with this new creature who was to be unique in nature and destiny.

The nature of this destiny is shown by the fact that God created Man in his own image and likeness. All creatures in this visible universe are like vestiges of the Creator; Man alone is his image. Moreover, at Man's creation, God placed him in the garden of Eden, which was also called the garden of Paradise.[15]

Eden in the ancient Akkadian (Babylonian) language meant "a plain." The scriptural account represents Eden, the first home of Man, as a park of trees, a beautiful oasis, abundantly watered,

---

[15] Gen. 4:16; 2:10.

contrasting sharply with the arid and barren earth that surrounded it[16] and upon which no rain had as yet fallen. There is no indication of the geographic "location of this primal habitat of Man, beyond placing it in the mysterious and remote east, a term which in Scripture signifies mystery.

A garden is of its very nature a place set apart for the exclusive use of its owner; it is not a public domain. The fact that God placed Adam in Eden in the very hour of his creation, in this domain of beauty, harmony, and peace, shows the singular nature of his destiny and the favor with which God regarded him.[17]

Eden itself may be regarded as a symbol of the Church on earth, for Scripture refers to the Church as "a garden enclosed,"[18] the place where God would dwell with Man and manifest his glory. Eden was likewise a symbolic counterpart of the Church in heaven, where God reveals his glory to the angelic creation, in the Beatific Vision. If we look deeply into the scriptural account of Eden, we shall find that it contains in itself, beneath the veil of symbol, the mystery of the whole human destiny, which constitutes the history of the Church on earth.

Reflecting upon this destiny as set forth in these opening chapters of Genesis, the Church says that Man was intended by God to be, not a mere creature or even a servant, but a son.[19] He was created to know, love, and serve God here on earth and, after his earthly life, to enjoy the unveiled vision of his glory forever in heaven. While abiding on earth, he was to be constituted lord of the universe.

---

[16] Cf. Gen. 2:4-14.
[17] Cf. Gen. 4:16.
[18] Cant. 4:12 (RSV = Song of Sol. 4:12).
[19] Cf. Rom. 8:15-17: Gal. 4:5-7.

Both his temporal and eternal destiny derived from the very nature of his being, which, in a sense, made him the soul of creation, for by reason of his rational nature, it was through him only that creation could ever know the Creator. Like the flame of the candle or the light of the lamp, he became the living spark that kindled the universe to rational life. He became, on behalf of creation, the mind that could know, the heart that could love, and the voice that could praise the Creator. It is understandable, therefore, that St. Paul spoke of creation as sharing in the tragedy of Man's Fall and eagerly awaiting his redemption.[20]

To equip Adam for his temporal and eternal destiny, God endowed him, at his creation, with a splendid hierarchy of gifts, both natural and supernatural. This hierarchy was necessary to him as the father of the human race. As the first parent of mankind, it was necessary that he be physically perfect; as the first and greatest human teacher, philosopher, and governor of the race, it was necessary that he be intellectually perfect; and as the first spiritual teacher of mankind, it was necessary that he be given the requisite spiritual gifts to fulfill this role.

In the gifts thus bestowed upon Man we can distinguish three types: natural, preternatural, and supernatural. A natural gift is an endowment proper to nature, as, for example, sight for the eyes. A preternatural gift is the enlargement of a natural gift, such as immortal life for the body. A supernatural gift is something above the nature of man; sanctifying grace and the Beatific Vision — that is, the face-to-face vision of God — are supernatural gifts.

In the natural order, God endowed Adam with physical integrity, which meant freedom from physical suffering, illness, and death. The crowning gift to this physical integrity was the preternatural

____

[20] Rom. 8:22.

gift of immortality. This meant that Man was destined to live for-ever in the integrity of his being, exempt from the law of death, which is the natural terminus of life in the universe.

True, Man's body was not naturally immortal, since it was made of substances that could be dissolved by natural forces, but just as God will give to the blessed soul, after the resurrection of all men, such a divine strength that it will be able to maintain the body im-mortal and incorrupt, so in the first creation of Man, God con-ferred upon the soul a supernatural force that would keep the body immortal as long as the soul was untainted by sin.

In addition to these physical gifts, God bestowed upon Adam the gift of a keen intellect with vast and profound powers of com-prehension. To begin with, his knowledge of God, while not su-pernatural, was so much superior to our knowledge of God that it could be called superhuman. He knew God more perfectly by far than we do, principally through his intelligible effects. With swift and facile comprehension, his mind ascended the ladder of wis-dom, from cause, order, purpose, plan as evident in creation, to the One in whom all these have their source. He did not have to pro-ceed step by step in his deductions, as we do. We could say that, in acquiring knowledge, our minds trudge along the way, but Adam's flew.

The intellectual endowments God bestowed upon him to fit him for his role as first human teacher have never been duplicated by any teacher since. Adam knew everything that can be known naturally, or, to express it in another way, he knew everything that a Man can know. His great powers of intellect can be better envis-aged if we remember that all knowledge is virtually contained in the relatively few self-evident principles out of which all under-standing proceeds and to which, conversely, all knowledge can be returned, Adam knew everything virtually contained in these principles. His knowledge of natural things was explicit, complete, and perfect. We might say that his mind was filled by God with divinely infused species through which he knew everything necessary for him to know, as the natural fount of all human wisdom.

On a supernatural plane, he knew at least some of the mysteries of faith. Such knowledge was necessary to him as the original preceptor of mankind, in view of the supernatural destiny that God willed for Man from the very moment of his creation. God would not assign a specific goal for Man and then expect him to attain it by accidently or unknowingly stumbling upon it. Recognizing the purpose of his life and of all human life, Adam was aware of the manner and means by which to fulfill such a purpose; this manner and these means were themselves supernatural. We can say, therefore, that Adam's knowledge extended to supernatural truths, those truths precisely which were necessary in order to direct life properly in its original state of integrity.

About other mysteries of faith, however, matters that cannot be apprehended by merely human efforts, he had no knowledge except that given him by divine revelation. He did not have knowledge, for example, of the essence of God. He did not see God as the blessed do in heaven, because this completely satisfying face-to-face awareness of divine Truth itself is infinitely above the capacity of any natural faculty. It is not even within the power of a preternatural or specially gifted mind such as we know Adam's was, because the knowledge of God that is obtained by seeing him face-to-face is a supernatural thing. This face-to-face vision would be God's final gift to Man, the gift of Beatitude, the understanding of God as he is in himself, but Man would have to earn that gift. Even in Eden, Adam did not understand God as he is in himself. Eden was still an earthly Paradise, a state of merit, and beyond it there was ultimately heaven.

The Mystery and Destiny of the Church

Another great gift God bestowed upon Adam at his creation was the natural law, engraved deep in his soul for the perfecting of his intellect and will. The natural law was like a compass designed to orient him toward God, the eternal truth and supreme good, the source and end of his being. This natural law is in itself a participation by creatures in the eternal law, each according to its nature. The eternal law, which is its source, is the divine wisdom insofar as it directs all creatures to their appointed end or goal in the Creator's design. From this eternal law are derived all other laws. Thus, the natural physical law is that branch of the eternal law which governs irrational creatures, while the natural moral law is that branch which governs rational creatures.

Like every other creature, Man is governed according to his nature; hence, the physical side of his nature is subject to the same physical laws that govern the animal kingdoms, but since God has destined him for a loftier vocation than these, and has for that reason endowed him with a rational nature, he has engraved indelibly upon his soul a natural inclination and power of intellect to know the truth and to distinguish good from evil. This special law is designed to guide and perfect rational nature, respecting his freedom as an intellectual being, unlike the natural physical law, which compulsively rules the animal creation.

The principles of the Natural Law in the heart of Man may be summed up as follows: to acknowledge a supreme being, to do good, to avoid evil, and to honor benefactors. It is this law which causes the insatiable yearning for God in the heart of Man, which incessantly urges him to seek, love, and possess that divine being who is the source and principle of his own.

We might compare this mysterious urge to the cosmic law of attraction by which the sun draws the planets to itself, and it is so deeply engraved upon Man's heart that no sophistication of culture or system of education can ever erase it. It is found in every race and civilization in every age, and it explains, on the one hand, why great natural virtue can be found in the lives of many who do not admit the existence of God and, on the other hand, why those who have led a life of sin will often, in their last moments, turn to God in sincere repentance. Such a final conversion is the soul's supreme attempt to ultimately make an irrevocable choice of the Infinite Good it was created to possess. The natural law might best be explained, perhaps, as the mysterious attraction by which God, the divine magnetic star, eternally draws the heart of Man to himself.

As the crown of all his gifts, God bestowed upon Man at his creation the gift of sanctifying grace. By reason of its transcendent nature, this gift is difficult to explain, being the supernatural life-principle of the soul of Man, as the soul itself is the life-principle of his body. The Church defines sanctifying grace as the communicated presence of God in the soul, a most mysterious, yet nonetheless very real presence. This divine communicated presence of God in the depths of Man's being suffuses his soul as light suffuses a prism, so that Man thereby becomes a living temple of God.

This indwelling presence of God in the soul of Man of its very nature raises him to a supernatural plane and enables him to live and operate on a plane that is above the deserts of his nature as a rational creature. It entitles him to move in a spiritual realm into which, according to his nature, he could never hope to enter. Jesus referred to this indwelling presence of God in the soul of Man when he said: "If anyone love me, he will keep my word and my Father will love him, and we will come to him and will make our abode with him."[21]

---

[21] John 14:23.

The first effect of sanctifying grace in the soul is that it gives Man a singular participated likeness to God. Man has now a two-fold likeness to God: the first, a natural likeness in the possession of a rational nature (intellect and free will); the second, a super-natural likeness, in the possession of the supernatural gift of sanctifying grace. St. Peter, in his second letter, actually said that it makes Man a partaker of the divine nature.[22]

This gift of sanctifying grace elevates Man to the dignity of an adopted son of God, and by this very fact, he acquires the right to inherit eternal life in the kingdom of heaven, in the enjoyment of the face-to-face vision of God's glory. For this reason, sanctifying grace is often referred to as the divine birthright of Man.

The effect of this gift of sanctifying grace on the soul of Man might be described as the effect of fire upon iron, or light passing through a prism, or the change wrought in the body of Jesus at the Transfiguration.[23] It clothes the soul with beauty and implants in the heart the seeds of virtue. In the possession of sanctifying grace, Man is made worthy to become the friend of God, worthy of his love and esteem. With this gift, Man's preparation by God for his appointed destiny was complete.

---

[22] Cf. 2 Pet. 1:4.
[23] Matt. 17; Mark 9; Luke 9:51.

Chapter 7

The Fall of Man

In his primal state of integrity, Adam was physically, morally, and intellectually a perfect Man. His excellence resulted from the perfect harmony of his nature, an internal orderliness that might be described as a chain of dependent subjections. Thus, his body was subject to his soul, his lower faculties were subject to the higher, and the higher were, in turn, subject to God. His nature was like a finely tuned instrument without the slightest breath of imperfection to mar its integrity, but the preservation of this integrity rested with Adam himself, for God would not thrust either himself or his gifts unwillingly upon his creature. Rather, in honor to his rational nature, he allowed Man to make his own free choice of accepting or rejecting him as his supreme good, the Friend and Benefactor to whom he owed all that he was and all that he had.

Sacred Scripture explicitly signifies that God placed our first parents on trial to allow them to make such a free choice. This trial is represented in Scripture as a Divine prohibition to eat the fruit of the Tree of Knowledge of Good and Evil. In essence, therefore, the divine precept forbade Man to sin, since the knowledge of good and evil in its fullest sense comprehends the whole moral law. Conversely it required that he adhere to God in friendship and holiness and acknowledge his sovereign dominion. The preservation of this state of primal integrity depended basically and ultimately on the subjection of his higher faculties to God. Because he had free will, his destiny was within his own power, for he could freely elect to abide by the divine precept or to reject it. As it turned out, he transgressed the command of God, being tempted thereto by the serpent, who persuaded him to do evil under the guise of good.[24]

Throughout the scriptural narrative, the tempter of our first parents is represented as a serpent. In her interpretation of this passage, however, the Church formally teaches that what appears in Genesis as "the serpent" is in reality the Devil, the leader of the fallen angels who is called elsewhere in Scripture Lucifer or Satan. We know from divine revelation that after he rebelled against God, he was cast out of heaven with the rebel angels but was permitted to enter the earth, where in due time he became the great adversary of Man.

His antagonism for mankind sprang from envy at seeing Man appointed to that destiny which he himself had forfeited through pride. It was of him that Jesus said: "He was a murderer from the beginning, and he stood not in the truth because the truth is not in him. When he speaks a lie, he speaks of his own, for he is a liar and the father thereof."[25]

In this first encounter with Man, he is represented as assuming the guise of a serpent, that creature which of its very nature is a natural symbol of deceitful cunning. In ancient pagan cults, it had become the symbol of immorality and for this reason was especially suited to the role of the tempter who, by his malicious insinuations, brought about the Fall of Man.

In accomplishing his design, he first led our first parents to question the motive of the divine prohibition, imputing it to jealousy

[24] Gen. 3:1-7.
[25] John 8:44.

The Fall of Man

on the part of God lest Man become like him, knowing good and evil. "No, you shall not die the death," he said, "for God knows that in what day soever you shall eat, your eyes shall be opened and you shall be as gods knowing good and evil."[26]

This lying assertion, presented as it was under the guise of good, was acceptable to Man, the spark that ignited his ambition to be like unto God. It was the same ambition that first urged the tempter himself to rebel in heaven. For it seemed to Man a greater good to be equal to God than to remain in his present status as a creature.

Of his own free choice, therefore, he transgressed the divine command in order to realize this ambition, and this ill-advised decision was his first sin. It is called by the Church *Original Sin* from the word *origin*, which means "beginning" or "source." It was in essence a sin of pride and disobedience to God, as St. Paul said: "By the disobedience of one Man, many were made sinners."[27]

Describing this first sin of Man, the inspired account says, "And the woman saw that the tree was good to eat and fair to the eyes and delightful to behold, and she took the fruit thereof and did eat and gave to her husband who did eat. And the eyes of them both were opened."[28] Having yielded to the deceitful suggestion of the tempter, they found only disillusionment and death; it is the psychology of all sin. Temptation to do evil, no matter whence it comes — whether from Man's own fallen nature or from the suggestion of the Devil — always presents itself under the guise of good. Like the fruit of the forbidden tree in Eden, it appears "good to partake of and fair to the eyes and delightful to behold," but

[26] Gen. 3:4-5.
[27] Rom. 5:19.
[28] Gen. 3:6-7.

once Man has yielded, his eyes are opened and he finds only the bitterness of death — that is, he experiences the remorse of sin.

The Divine judgment quickly followed upon Man's sin as God had forewarned,[29] for when Man refused to subject his higher faculties of intellect and will to God, the divinely bestowed hierarchy of gifts was destroyed. Thus, Adam, and in him the whole human race, fell from grace. The injury to Man's nature that resulted from the Fall, occurred essentially in the supernatural order, but it had repercussions on his entire nature, which was, so to speak, overcast by the dark shadow of sin as a sunlit landscape is overcast by dark storm clouds. In the material order, however, he suffered no natural loss to his nature in consequence of his Fall, since, naturally speaking, he was as much Man after his Fall as he was before.

The most important and immediate loss was the destruction of the supernatural life within his soul, the loss of sanctifying grace. This meant, in effect, that the communicated divine presence of God in his soul was withdrawn, and by that very fact, he had broken friendship with God. In the wake of this withdrawal, all his preternatural gifts vanished and the harmony that had reigned throughout his nature was permanently disrupted. On every level of his nature, he began to feel the effects of sin.

On the material level, he lost the integrity of his physical nature and became subject to suffering and death; on the intellectual level, his understanding was darkened and his will weakened. Thenceforth it was only by much labor of mind that he could acquire much of that knowledge which hitherto he could have easily apprehended, while in his moral nature he experienced a strong inclination to evil. As a result of these manifold defects, he quickly discovered that, whereas he was, by his very nature, fitted

[29] Cf. Gen. 2:17.

to be lord of the universe, he was now no longer master even of himself. He was like a bird with a broken wing, which, according to its nature, desires to fly upward but, by its infirmity, is constantly drawn downward.

Drawn toward God, the supreme good, by the very nature of his being, he now also experienced in himself an attraction to sin, so that he was constantly being torn in two directions: toward God and toward sin. St. Paul expressed this tragic consequence of sin when he said: "The good that I will, that I do not, but the evil which I will not, that I do . . . For I am delighted with the law of God, but I find in my members another law fighting against the law of my mind. Unhappy man that I am, who will deliver me from the body of this death?"[30]

These effects of sin were destined to be transmitted to the entire human race, since Adam was the father of all Mankind, as St. Paul again expressed it: "By one man sin entered the world and by sin, death, and so death passed upon all men, in whom all have sinned."[31] Indeed, the impress of this moral imbalance would be manifest on every page of human history throughout time.

On a spiritual plane, in the loss of sanctifying grace, he was deprived of his divine birthright, which entitled him to eternal life with God in the kingdom of heaven. This life of blessedness, enjoying the divine society of God's love and friendship in the glory of the Beatific Vision, implies much more than simply beholding God's glory from without, as it were. It implies, rather, the total immersion of Man's being in the infinite ocean of his mystery, so that, in contemplating the mystery of his divine being and life, his intellect reaches the fullness of its capacity for knowing while his

[30] Rom. 7:19, 22-24.
[31] Rom. 5:12.

will reaches the fullness of its capacity for loving, yet without exhausting the infinite ocean of mystery that it tries to sound.

Since only the infinite and incomprehensible ocean of God's being and nature can satisfy Man as a rational creature, he can reach the total fulfillment of his being only in the enjoyment of the Beatific Vision. For in possessing God, he will have come into the possession of the Infinite Good for which he was made. The magnitude of his loss of the gift of sanctifying grace, therefore, was beyond reckoning, for he could never hope to recover the privilege it accorded him by any effort of his own.

With the loss of sanctifying grace, he lost also the gift of immortality. This gift was like a precious fruit that he held in his hand but had not yet tasted, for it was to follow the completion of his earthly life, when, without having to experience death, he would be translated to eternal life. But before he could actually experience this gift, he fell from grace and was thus deprived of it.

The gift of immortality was clearly implied in the mystery of the Tree of Life in Eden and was also implicit in the divine precept not to eat of the fruit of the Tree of Knowledge: "In what day soever you shall eat of it, you shall die the death."[32] As regards the Tree of Life, the scriptural account seems to infer that it had a fruit of preternatural power, capable of entirely restoring human energy and vitality and, therefore, of preserving the strength of youth. By means of its fruit, our first parents, although mortal by nature, would have enjoyed the gift of immortality.

The withdrawal of this gift was signified by the divine judgment:

Behold, Adam is become as one of us, knowing good and evil: now, therefore, lest perhaps he put forth his hand and

[32] Gen. 2:17.

take also of the tree of life and eat and live forever. And the Lord God sent him out of the paradise of pleasure, to till the earth from which he was taken, and he placed before the paradise of pleasure Cherubims, and a flaming sword, turning every way, to keep the way of the tree of life.[33]

[33] Gen. 3:22-24.

Chapter 8

The Promise of Man's Redeemer

Thus bereft of his primal inheritance, Man stood in his impoverished nature before God. God could have abandoned Man and condemned him to abide forever in the state of alienation he had brought upon himself. Instead he willed to redeem him from the consequences of his sin, because, as St. Paul says, "the gifts and the calling of God are without repentance."[34]

So, even as he pronounced a sentence of just punishment upon the serpent who had deceived Man, God promised Man a Savior, one through whose mediation he would be reconciled to God and would recover his lost heritage. This formal promise of salvation was contained in the sentence of divine judgment upon the serpent: "I will put enmity between you and the woman, and your offspring and her offspring: she shall crush your head and you shall lie in wait for her heel."[35]

In her interpretation of this passage, the Church says that this divine judgment was a promise of salvation for mankind. The serpent is in reality the Devil; the woman in the immediate context signifies Eve, but in a prophetic and spiritual sense, she signifies the Woman of Destiny, the Mother of the Promised Savior. The woman's offspring in a particular sense signifies the Savior, but in a

[34] Rom. 11:29.
[35] Cf. Gen. 3:15.

general sense, it signifies all mankind. The offspring of the serpent signifies those who freely choose to follow Satan.

In promising a Savior to Man, God did not reveal his identity or the manner in which the redemption would be accomplished. He merely signified that the Savior would be a member of the human race, and that there would be perpetual enmity between him and the followers of Satan. It was only when he came that Man discovered who the Savior was — none other than the beloved Son of the eternal Father himself, who took to himself a human nature, of the Virgin Mary, that as God made Man, he might atone to the Father for the sins of Man by his death on the Cross. The eternal Father willed that the redemption of Man should be accomplished in this way, as Jesus signified to Nicodemus when he said:

> As Moses lifted up the serpent in the desert, so must the Son of Man be lifted up, that whosoever believes in him may not perish but may have life everlasting. For God so loved the world as to give his only-begotten Son: that whosoever believes in him may not perish but may have life everlasting. For God did not send his Son into the world to judge the world, but that the world may be saved by him.[36]

The Son himself assented to this design of the Father, and thus the mystery of Man's redemption came into being.

The taking of a human nature by the Son of God is called by the Church the mystery of the Incarnation — that is, the "becoming flesh." St. John the apostle explained the meaning of this mystery when he said: "And the Word was made flesh and dwelt among us, and we saw his glory, the glory that was his as the only

[36] John 3:13-17.

begotten of the Father, full of grace and truth."[37] Being both God and Man, he was a perfect mediator between God and Man, since he shared the nature of both the offended and the offender. As God, he could offer to the Father, on behalf of Man, an atonement for sin that would be worthy of his infinite majesty. As Man, his atonement would be truly human, and therefore a valid payment of Man's debt. Besides being an atonement offered by God's beloved Son, it would be worthy to reinstate Man in the Father's friendship.

The nature of the work of redemption was revealed to Joseph, who was betrothed to Mary, before the birth of Christ.

When the angel Gabriel was sent by God to dispel Joseph's doubt, he said to him: "Joseph, son of David, fear not to take unto you Mary your wife, for that which is conceived in her is of the Holy Spirit. And she shall bring forth a son: and you shall call his name JESUS. For he shall save his people from their sins."[38] St. John corroborated this testimony of the inspired evangelist when he said: "For this reason the Son of God appeared, that he might destroy the works of the Devil."[39]

It would pertain to the mission of Jesus as Savior to restore Man's primal destiny, his lost inheritance, and by the restoration of his divine birthright, which was sanctifying grace, to reopen to him the gates of heaven. In a word, he was to restore Man to the friendship of God, which he had lost by sin. Moreover, he was to give Man a way by which to live, which would be at once pleasing to God and deeply satisfying to himself. This way would teach him how to accommodate himself to the disabilities of his wounded

---

[37] John 1:14.
[38] Matt. 1:20-21.
[39] 1 John 3:8.

nature in such a manner as to secure his own self-fulfillment in the best possible way, and at the same time fulfill his deepest yearnings for happiness. This Way of life would be contained in the revelation he would bring to Man; the Church calls it the Gospel, or Good News, in contrast to the decree of divine punishment which followed immediately upon Man's sin. In Sacred Scripture, it is frequently referred to as the promise.[40]

The mystery of the Incarnation of the Son of God is the center and focal point of human history, for the whole mystery of the human destiny revolves around the fact of Man's redemption by God. The entrance of Jesus into the orbit of human history stands at the center of time, for he is like a center of gravitation, which draws the mystery of the human destiny to himself. For him all time was made, as he himself said in his prayer to the Father at the Last Supper: "All my things are thine, and thine are mine, and I am glorified in them.[41] His presence fills the entire mystery of time as the coordinating element of human history. Without his presence, the events of human history are like the disjointed pieces of a jigsaw puzzle that cannot be fitted together. In the light of his presence, however, human history reveals that marvelous harmony of design which is characteristic of all the works of God.

For ever since God promised a Redeemer to Man, Jesus was present in the world, beneath the veils of symbol and prophecy, until, at the time appointed by the Father, he took a human nature to himself and walked among men.[42] We could say that he traversed the highway of the ages with wayfaring Man, just as he

---

[40] Gal. 3:16 ff.

[41] John 17:10.

[42] Cf. John 5:39-47; Luke 24:25-27, 44-48; cf. Bar. 3:33; John 1:14.

walked the road to Emmaus with the two disciples on the day of his Resurrection, and the evolution of the human destiny reveals him as the Lord of history, the King of the ages, and the Savior of all mankind. The Church says that the primal Promise of Eden reached its fulfillment in Christ. In this connection, it is interesting to note that when the angel announced his birth to the shepherds of Bethlehem, he said: "Fear not, for behold I bring you good tidings of great joy, that shall be to all the people, for this day is born to you a Savior, who is Christ the Lord, in the city of David."[43]

There were many ways in which God could have decreed the redemption of Man; why he chose that way is the secret of his own Divine counsel. The Church says that it may have been in order to bring Man to a realization of the nature and malice of sin, as also to convince him of God's incomparable love for him. For Man, by his nature, tends to measure spiritual realities by external signs, and this is especially true in regard to love. The glory of God's works might leave him in awe of the divine majesty, but they would not necessarily move him to love; but the realization that God so loved him as to will the death of his only beloved Son, in order to save him from his misery, could not fail to evoke a response of love.

So let us look at fallen Man as he set forward on his pilgrimage through time to achieve his temporal and eternal destiny.

[43] Luke 2:10-11.

Chapter 9

Man's Destiny

In one of his verbal conflicts with the Pharisees, Jesus once said: "My Father works until now, and I work."[44] He was referring to the Father's providence over creation, in particular over Man, as it is revealed in the unfolding of Salvation History.

With the creation of Man, the evolution of the human destiny began, as it begins for each individual at his birth. Considered from a historical point of view, the unfolding of the human destiny constitutes the record of secular history, from a theological point of view, it forms the record of Salvation History. We might say that secular and salvation history stand in relation to each other as two concentric circles revolving around the mystery of Man, the larger and outer circle representing Salvation History, the smaller and inner circle representing secular history. For Salvation History embraces the entire destiny of Man from the beginning until the end of time.

From whichever standpoint we view it, the history of Man is unique, for while the inanimate universe and the plant and animal kingdoms have their own particular "history," the history of Man differs radically from both of them, being far more complex and profound. This is so because, by reason of his rational nature, the history of Man involves not only the record of his material

[44] Cf. John 5:17.

achievements but that of his intellectual and spiritual development as well.

Since, in the divine plan of salvation, the promised redeemer was destined to be the center of human history, we find the key to the checkered pattern of human events from the beginning in the mystery of Christ. Knowingly or unknowingly, every age that preceded him looked forward to his coming and was in some way, directly or indirectly, remotely or proximately involved in God's preparation of the world for it; likewise every age that followed him looks back to find its true significance in him. His mystery fills all time: he fulfills all prophecy; he dominates all history and involves all ages and nations in his salvation.

Considering the whole mystery of the human destiny in the light of this divine plan, it is interesting to investigate what design Salvation History presents in the light of his presence. When it is examined in relation to Jesus, we could say that the entire record of human history falls into seven distinct ages of time, which we might describe as the Seven Days of the Week of Salvation History.

The book of Genesis portrays God accomplishing the work of creation in a week of six days followed by a Sabbath rest: likewise Sacred Scripture reveals him accomplishing his plan of redemption for Man during a week of six days — the week of Salvation History which will be followed by the Sabbath Day of eternal life.[45]

The first two days of this Salvation Week are self-evident from Scripture: from Adam to Noah and from Noah to Abraham. St. Matthew gives us the next three in the very first chapter of his Gospel: from Abraham to David, from David to the Babylonian

---

[45] Cf. Heb. 3:1-6; 4:1-11.

Captivity, and from the Babylon Captivity to Christ.[46] Jesus, by his coming, inaugurated the Sixth Day of the Salvation Week, which will last until the end of time, after which will follow the Seventh Day of eternal life, the eternal Sabbath rest. Thus, the entire mystery of Salvation History could be written as the calendar of a seven-day week, as follows:

THE WEEK OF SALVATION HISTORY

First Day: From Adam to Noah
Second Day: From Noah to Abraham
Third Day: From Abraham to David
Fourth Day: From David to Babylon
Fifth Day: From Babylon to Christ
Sixth Day: From Christ to the end of time
Seventh Day: From the end of time to all eternity

At the dawn of each Day of this Salvation Week stands an event of great importance in the history of mankind, one that is destined to have profound and far-reaching implications for the Church in future ages, for each signals a new phase in the unfolding of human history.

Thus, at the dawn of the First Day stands the drama of Man's creation, his Fall, and God's promise of redemption. At the dawn of the Second Day stands God's covenant with Noah and the blessing of Shem, his eldest son, which marked the foundation of the race from which the Promised Savior would come. At the dawn of the Third Day stands the Call of Abraham, who was destined to become the father of the Chosen People, the nation of which the Savior was to be born. At the dawn of the Fourth Day stands the

---

[46] Matt. 1:17.

anointing of David as king over Israel, the one who was destined to be the founder of the royal dynasty of the Savior. At the dawn of the Fifth Day stands the great Babylonian Captivity or Exile, which was God's final preparation of his people for the coming of the Savior. At the dawn of the Sixth Day stands the birth of Christ, the Promised Savior, the focal point of all human history, which alone gives cohesion and meaning to the mystery of the human destiny. At the dawn of the Seventh Day stands the Second Coming of Christ, the event that will signal the consummation of the human destiny on earth and the translation of the Church to eternal life in heaven. This will mark the final achievement of Man's destiny.

The mystery of the Church has a twofold aspect, for it involves, on the one hand, the mysterious action of God in the world in every age, ordering all events and circumstances toward a determined goal for his own eternal glory, and, on the other hand, the manifold activities of Man, both on a material and a spiritual plane. The continuous interweaving of this divine and human action constitutes the mystery of the Church on earth.

It is evident from Sacred Scripture that, from the moment God promised salvation to Man and willed the nature of that salvation, he never ceased to work toward its accomplishment. His work in bringing the plan of redemption to fulfillment is revealed in the Scriptures under various aspects.

Thus, he is described as a householder who went forth to the field in the springtime, to cast the seed of future redemption into the earth and to preside over its growth until it sprang up and became a living reality in the mystery of Christ. Jesus himself referred to this divine activity of the Father when he said: "So is the kingdom of God, as if a Man should cast seed into the earth and should sleep and rise night and day, and the seed should spring up and grow while he knows it not. For the earth of itself brings forth fruit, first the blade, then the ear, and afterward the full corn in the ear. And when the fruit is brought forth, immediately he puts in the sickle because the harvest is come."[47]

God's promise to send a Savior to Man was the grain cast into the earth in the springtime of the world, its springing up was the coming of Christ, and its harvest was the mystery of redemption.

Again the Scriptures portray God as the Lord of a vineyard, over which he presides throughout the day of time,[48] or as a householder who prepared a supper for his guests at the close of day.[49] All of these symbols were intended to focus the attention of the faithful upon the consummation of the mystery of the Church in some distant age. Meanwhile, Man had to traverse the great highway of the ages beneath the watchful eye of God, and it will be deeply interesting to contemplate him as he walks down the path of time, the wayfaring pilgrim of the ages.

---

[47] Mark 4:26-29.
[48] Cf. Matt. 20.
[49] Cf. Luke 14:16.

Chapter 10

The Mystery of Eden

When we reflect upon the mystery of Eden, we can see beneath the veil of symbol and prophecy the whole plan of redemption, from the formal sentence of divine judgment upon the serpent, to the final triumph of the Promised Savior by the mystery of the Cross: "I will put enmity between you and the woman, and your offspring and her offspring. She shall crush your head, and you shall lie in wait for her heel." As we now know, the Woman of Destiny was Mary, the Mother of Jesus, the Promised Savior. Ages later St. John beheld her in vision on the island of Patmos, clothed with the sun, with the moon beneath her feet, and upon her head a crown of twelve stars.[50] This cosmic scene graphically portrayed the nature and dimension of Mary's vocation in the Church, for it was through Jesus, her son, that the serpent's head would be crushed in the mystery of redemption, indeed the Church herself says that God's primal promise of salvation would be fulfilled in Christ.[51]

The grace of salvation was foreshown in the mysterious spring that arose in Eden and, dividing into four rivers, flowed forth to water the whole earth; it was an apt symbol of Christ.[52]

---

[50] Cf. Apoc. 12:1 (RSV = Rev. 12:1).

[51] Cf. Matt. 1:21, 28:18-20; Mark 16:15-20; Luke 24:25-27, 44-53; John 20:19-23; 21; Acts 4:11-1.

[52] Cf. John 7:37-39; 4:14.

The Mystery and Destiny of the Church

The prophet Ezekiel beheld a mystic river issuing forth from beneath the door of the Temple, and thence flowing away toward the east, to bring life to every creature with which it came into contact.[53] It assumed a concrete and visible dimension, so to speak, in the river Jordan, which symbolized it, and its waters were thus sanctified by the Baptism of Jesus. The Holy Spirit signified what this mystic river symbolized when, through the inspired writer, he showed it to be a symbol of the Savior and his salvation. Thus, the Sacred Scriptures depict Jesus, the Eternal Wisdom of the Father, coming down from heaven, the celestial Eden, to inundate the whole earth like a mighty river with the waters of the grace of redemption.

Describing this mystic inundation, the inspired writer said:

> I, wisdom, have poured out rivers; I, like a brook out of a river of mighty water; I, like a channel of a river, and like an aqueduct, came out of paradise. And I said I will water my garden of plants, and I will water abundantly the fruits of my meadow. And behold my brook became a great river, and my river came near to a sea. For I make doctrine to shine forth to all as the morning light: and I will declare it afar off. I will yet pour out doctrine as prophecy, and will leave it to them that seek wisdom. See that I have not labored for myself only, but for all that seek out the truth.[54]

Jesus revealed the nature of the waters of this mystic river of Eden to the Samaritan woman by Jacob's well, when he said to her:

> Whosoever drinks of this water shall thirst again, but he that shall drink of the water that I shall give him shall not thirst

---

[53] Ezek. 47:1-9.
[54] Cf. Ecclus. 24:40-47 (RSV = Sir. 24:30-34).

forever. But the water that I will give him shall become in him a fountain of water, springing up into life everlasting.[55]

Lastly, the Tree of Life, in a prophetic and spiritual sense, signified the Cross, the very instrument of redemption by means of which Man would ultimately regain his lost inheritance.

After the Fall, Man was forbidden access to the Tree of Life in Eden, lest he live forever,[56] but with the redemption this divine prohibition was reversed, and he was bidden to approach the true Tree of Life, that by partaking of its fruit, he might truly possess life everlasting. Jesus said:

> I am the bread of life. He that eats of this bread shall live forever, for the bread that I shall give is my flesh, for the life of the world. I solemnly assure you: except you eat the flesh of the Son of Man and drink his blood, you shall not have life in you. He that eats my flesh and drinks my blood has everlasting life, and I will raise him up on the last day.[57]

We see from this that if we look deeply into the mystery of Eden, we shall find that it contains in essence the entire destiny of Man beneath the veil of prophetic symbol, and we shall encounter therein all the fundamental doctrines of the Christian Faith.

Thus, in the story of Eden we first meet the living God, the source and first principle of Man's being, and of all creation. We encounter, too, the mystery of the Church in heaven, in the person of the angels at the gates of Paradise, and the mystery of the Church on earth in the person of our first parents. Implicit in this revelation is the doctrine of the Communion of Saints, which

[55] John 4:13-14.
[56] Gen. 3:22-24.
[57] Cf. John 6:48, 52, 54-55 (RSV = John 6:48, 51, 53-54).

unites the Church in heaven with that on earth in one common destiny. We encounter the mystery of evil and of hell, in the presence of the serpent, the Devil, who tempted our first parents to sin, and we encounter the mystery of sin in the Tree of Knowledge of Good and Evil.

We encounter Jesus, the Son of God, in the promised Savior, and implicit in this promise is the presence of the Holy Spirit, by whom the mystery of the Incarnation of the only-begotten Son of the eternal Father would be accomplished in time. And thus we meet in Eden the mystery of the triune God, Father, Son, and Holy Spirit.

In the promise of a Savior, furthermore, we implicitly encounter the whole mystery of redemption; and implicit also in this promise is the doctrine of the forgiveness of sin.

Then again, in this primal promise of salvation we meet for the first time Mary, the virgin mother of Jesus. And lastly, in Eden we encounter Man's ultimate destiny, which is the mystery of eternal life with God, hidden beneath the symbol of the Tree of Life. And implicit in this revelation is the doctrine of the resurrection of the body. Thus, we see that every article of Faith contained in the Apostles' Creed is hidden within the story of Eden. Indeed, we could safely say that all subsequent revelation given to Man by God was a development of that primal revelation of Eden.

When, after the Fall, Man stood in his impoverished nature before God, he was still, even in his fallen state, the object of the Father's providence and love. In a natural sense, he was still the lord of creation, appointed by God to rule and subdue the universe, but now he had to bring to this work of conquest a darkened intellect and a weakened will. His temporal destiny remained the same, but his spiritual destiny was vastly changed, because now he was in a state of alienation from God. As he set forward on his journey

through time, however, he was all unknowingly guided on his way
by the Father's providence, for he was still regarded by the Father
as his child, even though, as a result of Man's sin, the Father had
hidden his face from him. The subsequent unfolding of his destiny
would form the record of Salvation History.

With the casting forth of our first parents from Eden, the opening chapter of human history was closed and the blueprint of the
human destiny was completed. It was in Eden that Man first en-
countered the Redeemer who was henceforth to walk with him
along the highway of the ages, beneath the veils of symbol and
prophecy, until he took flesh and dwelt among us in the mystery
of his Incarnation.[58] From divine revelation we know that his
mystery fills all time and all eternity,[59] because, before he became
Man at his Incarnation, he existed as God from all eternity, consubstantial and co-eternal with the Father in the unity of the Holy
Spirit, in the mystery of the Triune God. It was he who said of himself through the inspired writer:

> The Lord possessed me in the beginning of his ways, before
> he made anything from the beginning. I was set up from
> eternity, and of old before the earth was made. The depths
> were not as yet, and I was already conceived; neither had
> the fountains of waters as yet sprung out. The mountains
> with their huge bulk had not as yet been established; before
> the hills I was brought forth. He had not yet made the earth,
> nor the rivers, nor the poles of the world. When he pre-
> pared the heavens, I was present when, with a certain law
> and compass, he enclosed the depths; when he established
> the sky above, and poised the fountains of waters; when he

[58] Cf. Bar. 3:38.
[59] 2 Paralip. 6:18 (RSV = 2 Chron. 6:18).

compassed the sea with its bounds, and set a law to the waters that they should not pass their limits; when he balanced the foundations of the earth, I was with him, forming all things . . . Now, therefore, ye children, hear me: Blessed are they that keep my ways. He that shall find me shall find life, and shall have salvation from the Lord. But he that shall sin against me shall hurt his own soul. All that hate me love death.[60]

St. John, in the opening chapter of his Gospel, made a formal declaration of the eternal generation of Christ in his divine nature from the eternal Father. He said:

In the beginning was the Word, and the Word was with God, and the Word was God. The same was in the beginning with God. All things were made by him: and without him was made nothing that was made. And the Word was made flesh, and dwelt among us, and we saw his glory, the glory as it were of the only-begotten of the Father, full of grace and truth.[61]

This is the one whom we honored in the Great Jubilee that opened the third millennium, whose mystery fills time and history, and alone gives the human destiny both cohesion and meaning.

He has walked with Man since the days of Eden, and he shall continue to walk with him until he achieves the consummation of his destiny in the mystery of eternal life, as he himself signified to his Apostles before he ascended into heaven: "Behold I am with you all days, even to the consummation of the world."[62]

---

[60] Prov. 8:22-36.
[61] John 1:1-3, 14.
[62] Matt. 28:20.

Part 3

The Week of Salvation History

Chapter 11

Man: Pilgrim of the Ages

As Man set forth on his journey through time, the great vista of the ages stretched out before him into the distant future until its ultimate perspectives were mingled with the mystery of eternity. This was the time allotted him by God to achieve his destiny. Materially speaking, his journey was to take him to the ends of the earth and even beyond, into the realms of outer space. Intellectually it was to take him from the Stone Age to the Space Age. Spiritually it was to take him from the shadow of this earthly existence to the vision of God, the eternal reality, in whose likeness he is made. The story of his journey through time, as it evolved in the Seven Days of Salvation History, is the story of the Church on earth.

From the very outset, as we have said, the effects of Original Sin were manifest in his nature. One important result of the Fall was the fact that Man lost his primal knowledge of God, although he did not and could not lose his natural hunger for him: before that could come to pass, he would have had to change his nature. But no longer knowing God, he began to worship instead the work of God's hands, and thus idolatry became widespread in the ancient world. Yet this very idolatry revealed the mysterious attraction by which God eternally draws the heart of Man to himself. For it clearly showed that in every age, Man was seeking God, although he could not find him.

The Mystery and Destiny of the Church

On a moral plane, the effects of Original Sin were also evident, for the conflict between good and evil was ever present, resulting all too often in the triumph of evil. Thus, in his fallen nature, with a darkened understanding and a weakened will, having lost his authentic knowledge of God and even of his own destiny, Man immersed himself in the things of time, and in the building of the earthly city. Nothing better, perhaps, betrays his incessant preoccupation with the city of Man than the story of Babel.[63] Yet while immersed in his secular pursuits, he was all unknowingly being used by God, the Architect of creation, as a living stone in the building of the City of God.

Any survey of Salvation History reveals that every nation on earth, knowingly or unknowingly, actively or passively had a part to play in the mystery of redemption, since it was a matter for the entire human race. Many of the great civilizations of antiquity had a highly important role to play in the great drama of redemption, although they were totally unaware of it at the time. All others were passively awaiting redemption as the flock awaits its shepherd or the harvest its reaper, and thus, the mystery of the human destiny evolved through the ages beneath the watchful eye of God.

The Divine activity in the ordering of this evolution during the ages that preceded the coming of the Savior might be called the Church in Preparation. The activity of Jesus, the Savior himself, in founding his Church, when he actually came, might be called the Church in her establishment, while the final translation of the Church to eternal life at the end of time might be called the Church in her consummation.

Because it is a mystery of many facets, the Church has been compared to many things in an effort to explain her nature. Thus,

[63] Gen. 11:1-9.

it has been compared to the day that endures from dawn to sunset, the only difference being that the mystery of the Church will know no sunset but will end rather in eternal day. Again as we have said, it has been compared to a field planted by God in the springtime of the world and growing toward the harvest at the end of time: like the growing field, it presents a different aspect in every age. Yet again, it has been compared to a ship sailing toward a distant shore, or a pilgrim faring toward a distant homeland.

If we stand by the wayside of time and watch the pageant of the ages slowly passing by, we can see the Church during its period of preparation, like a beautiful tapestry being woven by God from the varied threads of human history into an eternal design of his glory, or a great symphony in which the divergent elements of human history, with its joy and sorrow, its pain and tragedy, were all being harmonized into a beautiful hymn to his glory. Or again, we can see it as a great drama being played out upon the stage of time since the dawn of history, the climactic scene of which was the entrance of Christ, the Son of God, into the world as Man, to be its Savior.

His First Coming was destined to have profound implications for every member of the human race, and all ages and nations were to be made one in his mystery. His Second Coming will mark the closing of the book of human destiny.

St. John, in his vision on Patmos, saw the mystery of this final consummation, when Man, having completed his pilgrimage through time, will have finally entered into his rest to enjoy the face-to-face vision of God in the glory of eternal life. Describing his vision he said:

> I saw a great multitude which no Man could number, of all nations and tribes and tongues and peoples, standing before

the throne of God, in the sight of the Lamb, clothed with white robes and having palms in their hands. And all the angels stood around about the throne, and the ancients and the four living creatures: and they fell down before the throne and adored God, saying: "Amen. Benediction and glory and wisdom and thanksgiving and honor and power and strength be to our God forever and ever."

And one of the ancients said to me: "These that are clothed in white robes — who are they and from whence did they come?" And I said to him: "My lord, you know." And he said to me: "These are they who have come out of great tribulation and have washed their robes and made them white in the blood of the Lamb. Therefore they are before the throne of God and they serve him day and night in his temple."

And he who sits on his throne shall dwell over them. They shall no more hunger nor thirst, neither shall the sun fall on them, nor any heat, for the Lamb who is in the midst of the throne shall rule over them and shall lead them to the fountains of the waters of life. And God shall wipe away all tears from their eyes . . . and death shall be no more nor mourning nor crying, nor sorrow shall be anymore, for the former things are passed away." And he that sat on the throne said: "Behold, I make all things new."

And he [the angel] showed me a river of the water of life, clear as crystal, proceeding from the throne of God and of the Lamb. In the midst of the street of the city and on both sides of the river was the Tree of Life, bearing twelve fruits every month; and the leaves of the tree were for the healing of the nations. And there shall be no curse anymore, but the throne of God and of the Lamb shall be in the city, and his servants shall serve him and they shall see his face and his name shall be on their foreheads. And night shall be no more. And they shall not need the light of the lamp nor the light of the sun because the Lord God shall enlighten them and they shall reign forever and ever.[64]

The Tree of Life signified the Cross of Jesus, and the Twelve Fruits, the consummation of the mystery of redemption in the fruition of eternal life.

From these considerations we see that the evolution of the human destiny, whether considered as secular or sacred history, when viewed in the light of divine revelation, presents a marvelous harmony of design. Indeed, it is faith alone that supplies the authentic key to the riddle of human existence and unlocks the mystery of the human destiny.

In the following chapters we shall consider the events of the Week of Salvation History at greater length.

---

[64] Cf. Apoc. 7:9-17; 21:4-5; 22:1-5 (RSV = Rev. 7:9-17; 21:4-5; 22:1-5).

Chapter 12

The First Day: From Adam to Noah

Historically speaking, the entire record of human history falls into two basic divisions — namely, the historic and the prehistoric periods of mankind. In point of time, there is no comparison between the two, for the prehistoric period is of immense duration, embracing the entire era of human history from the first appearance of Man until the beginning of the historic period, about ten thousand years ago.

Whether in secular or sacred history, the prehistoric period of Man constitutes the first chapter of the human story. In secular history, it is usually referred to as the Stone Age; in sacred history, it covers the period from Adam to Noah, which is recorded in the first eleven chapters of Genesis.

The historic period is subdivided into smaller epochs. We might say, therefore, that the prehistoric period of Man constitutes the First Day of the Week of Salvation History, while the subdivisions of the historic period could be regarded as the remaining days of the Salvation Week. This is just one possible way of dividing up the entire record of human history. The general line of demarcation between these two basic periods of Man's history is usually considered to be the Great Deluge described in the seventh chapter of the book of Genesis.

As regards the First Day of the Week of Salvation History — that is, the prehistoric day of Man — we know very little. Even considered from a point of view of secular history, our knowledge of that primal epoch is scant and fragmentary. This is due not only to its great remoteness in time but also to the absence of any written records during that period. Whether any such ever existed is not known. Scholars are generally of the opinion that they did not, since Man probably had not invented the art of writing at that time; and even if he had, it is unlikely that any written records could have survived through so many ages.

Our knowledge of that primal day of Man is therefore very limited, but what evidence we possess is irrefutable, being enshrined in the geological strata of the earth. Thus, we know, for example, that during that primal age, the human race had spread probably over the entire earth, for traces of the very first civilizations have been discovered in the far-flung regions of the world. The geological evidence of Man's presence, moreover, during that exceedingly remote age, reveals that he was very much like the Man of today. The tools he used, the weapons he fashioned, the arts and crafts of life he gradually developed all bear eloquent testimony to this fact.

An interesting feature of this First Day, is the great age assigned to men in both sacred and secular history. Kings and patriarchs were reputed to have lived for several hundred years. Explaining this curious fact, exegetes are agreed today that these ages are not to be understood as a chronological reckoning of time; rather, they are most probably theological or symbolic.

As regards Man's moral history during this first age, our only source of information is what is contained in the scriptural record. From the book of Genesis we learn that moral decadence was so widespread and depraved that God repented of having made Man, and he sent the Flood as a divine chastisement for sin. This Flood described in the book of Genesis is the first recorded catastrophe in human history. That it actually occurred cannot reasonably be doubted, for there is a global tradition of this event among all peoples. Scholars and exegetes today are generally agreed that the great epic of Gilgamish, of the ancient Babylonian story of the Deluge, describes the same event as that recorded in Genesis. Neither account is dependent on the other, but both go back to a common source.

Scientists today are reluctant to assign any specific date to the Flood, beyond a general statement that it occurred at the very dawn of the historic period of Man. Its natural cause is unknown, but such an inundation could have occurred as a result of abrupt changes in temperature at the end of an ice age. Whether it involved a complete or only a partial inundation cannot be established with certainty from the scriptural account, because the record in Genesis might be figurative rather than factual. Thus, the total submersion implied in the story of the Deluge may in actual fact have signified only a catastrophe of considerable dimension. Instances of this figurative mode of speech are frequently found in Scripture, as, for example, when the Gospel says that a decree "went out from Caesar Augustus that the whole world should be enrolled."[65] The "whole world" signified merely the Roman Empire.

The geographical extent of the Deluge is relatively unimportant; what is supremely important is the theological truth the story is meant to convey — namely, that sin is inevitably punished by God. Man as a rational creature cannot with impunity continue in evil, for there comes an ultimate reckoning. Yet the divine chastisement is always intended for his correction, not for his destruction, as is evident from the story of the Flood. God chastised Man by means of the Flood, but he saved him by means of the Ark.

[65] Luke 2:1.

As savior of the ancient world, Noah was a figure of Christ, the Savior of the human race. Guiding the Ark over the waters, he prefigured Christ, who guides the Church over the turbulent waters of time to the shores of eternal life. The Ark itself was a prophetic figure of the Church, which is called in Scripture the "Ark of salvation." According to St. Peter, it was also a figure of Christian Baptism.[66]

From these considerations we can see that at the very dawn of recorded history, God gave to mankind, in this mysterious event, a preview of the mystery of salvation. The Deluge brought to a close the great prehistoric period of Man, and thus ended the First Day of the Week of Salvation History.

[66] Cf. 1 Pet. 3:18-22.

Chapter 13

The Second Day: From Noah to Abraham

The Second Day of the Salvation Week is that period of indeterminate length which followed upon the great Flood and ended with the Call of Abraham, being at least about two thousand years in duration. This epoch marks the historic period of Man, the opening of the second chapter of the human story.

This was the springtime of the Salvation Year, when God went forth into the field of the world to sow the seeds of a harvest that he would reap in distant ages to come. It was a very important Day in the history of salvation, for God was at work on both a natural and a supernatural plane, ordering all things toward the development of his redemptive plan for mankind; and it is interesting to note that during this Day, he was using the temporal achievements of Man to further the designs of his glory.

His covenant with Noah after the Flood ushered in this Second Day of Salvation History. This covenant was a renewal of the primal promise of hope given to our first parents after the Fall. The sign of the covenant was the rainbow, a symbol of the divine all-embracing fidelity and love that would enfold mankind in every future age. God's blessing of Shem, Noah's eldest son, marked the foundation of the race of which the promised Savior would come.

In the sphere of secular history, this age saw the growth and development of what we might call the human family tree, in the establishment of the great basic races of mankind — namely, the

Semitic, Hamitic, and Japhetic races, sprung from the three sons of Noah. This age also witnessed the rise of the various ethnic and cultural groups of the ancient world; and the great civilizations of remote antiquity came into being. Chief among these civilizations were those of ancient Babylon and Egypt, which flourished contemporaneously, and which stand at the very dawn of the Historic Day of Man, revealing his intellectual genius in every sphere of life — social, economic and intellectual. These two civilizations had a highly important role to play in the history of salvation.

Babylon at this time became a politically unified nation with a codified system of law. Gradually it extended its dominions, thus bringing the subjugated nations of the surrounding regions under the refining influence of its culture. Trade and commerce flourished, and the arts were assiduously cultivated. It was in ancient Babylon that the art of writing was first developed and perfected.

Like Babylon, Egypt developed a splendid culture of its own. Fully three thousand years before the coming of Christ, it was a strong and unified nation. The primal period of its culture was divided into three distinct periods: the early, the middle, and the late. From about the year 3000 BC until the fifth century before Christ, the nation counted thirty-one ruling dynasties, the supreme ruler being called Pharaoh.

Also like Babylon, Egypt carried on an extensive trade and commerce; cultivated the arts, especially sculpture, painting, and woodcarving; and became renowned for the magnificence of its architecture. The pyramids were built in the most ancient period of its culture. It had its own calendar, which closely approximated our solar calendar, having 365 days. The observance of the Sothic Period, a cycle of 1,456 years, based on the heliacal rising of the star Sotis, also bore eloquent testimony to the intellectual genius of that far distant age. Although too vast to be of use as an ordinary calendar, the Sothic Period is of great value to scholars in helping to place dates of ancient Egyptian history accurately.

In retrospect, the predestined roles of these two ancient civilizations in Salvation History become apparent. It was from the rock of ancient Babylon that the nation of Israel, in the person of Abraham, was hewn,[67] and it was likewise in that land long ages later, that the Chosen People spent seventy years in exile, as a final preparation for their predestined role in Salvation History as the people of the Redeemer. That event, commonly known as the Babylonian Captivity, occurred only five centuries before Jesus came.

Egypt, too, later in its history, was linked by a mysterious destiny to Israel, for it was in that land that the Chosen People dwelt in exile for 430 years[68] and suffered a cruel enslavement at the hands of the Pharaohs. There they became a great nation, and from there they were finally led forth to freedom by Moses. In the unfolding of their destiny in Egypt and the events of the Exodus under Moses, God gave mankind a silent preview of the whole mystery of redemption, beneath the veil of symbol and prophetic type.

Then, long ages after these great civilizations had flourished, those of Greece and Rome sprang up from them as from an ancient root, and these also were destined by God to play a role of imponderable magnitude in the mystery of salvation. They were, in fact, the divinely chosen instruments by which the gospel of salvation would be brought to the ends of the earth. From these considerations it is evident that the seeds of future harvest sown by God in this remote age bore fruit in the mystery of redemption. This Second Day of the Week of Salvation History closed with the Call of Abraham.

[67] Cf. Isa. 51:1.
[68] Exod. 12:40.

Chapter 14

The Third Day: From Abraham to David

The Third Day of the Salvation Week began with the Call of Abraham by God about the year 1850 BC, and it endured for about eight centuries, closing with the anointing of David as king over Israel about the year 1010 BC. The Call of Abraham is the first date in Salvation History that can be placed with a fair degree of probability, and this event was destined to have vast and profound repercussions on the Church in all subsequent ages, for it witnessed the institution of the nation and people of the promised Redeemer in the person of Abraham. It is therefore a Day of consummate importance for the Church.

It is St. Matthew who delineated this and the two following Days of the Salvation Week, in the first chapter of his Gospel.[69] He divided the entire history of Israel prior to the coming of Christ into three parts — namely, from Abraham to David, from David to the Babylon Captivity, and from the Babylon Captivity to Christ. This division was symbolic rather than mathematical, yet it is deeply significant in the light of Salvation History, for it supplies the Third, Fourth, and Fifth Days of the Salvation Week.

The dawn of this Third Day marked the opening of the third chapter in the human story, for God's choice of Abraham to be the father of the Chosen People invested him with a unique vocation

[69] Matt. 1:17.

in the Church. Of this people the Savior was to come. This Day, therefore, was important not only for the destiny of Israel, but for that of the Gentile nations as well.

It dawned when God called Abraham, saying: "Go forth out of your country and from your kindred, and out of your Father's house and come into the land which I will show you; and I will make of you a great nation . . . and in you shall all the kindreds of the earth be blessed."[70] Obedient to the divine call, Abraham left the affluence and culture of his native region and, as Scripture says, "went forth in faith, not knowing whither he went . . . for he looked for a city that has foundations, whose builder and maker is God."[71]

Having chosen him for this predestined vocation, God made a covenant with him, the sign of which was circumcision, promising to do all that he had said, and that through his son Isaac all these divine promises would be fulfilled. But no sooner had he made this covenant than he asked Abraham to sacrifice the very son through whom he promised to fulfill all that he had said.

Never doubting God's truth and fidelity, the patriarch prepared to sacrifice his son Isaac, in obedience to the divine command; but as he was about to slay him, God bade him desist, because he did not will the death of the boy; he was merely testing Abraham's faith and obedience. So greatly was he pleased with the patriarch's fidelity that he confirmed all his former promises with an oath. He said:

> By my own self have I sworn, because you have done this thing, and have not spared your only-begotten son for my sake: I will bless you and I will multiply your descendants as the stars of heaven and as the sand which is on the seashore.

[70] Cf. Gen. 12:1-3.
[71] Heb. 11:8, 10.

And your descendants shall possess the gates of your enemies. And in your descendants shall all the nations of the earth be blessed; because you have obeyed my voice.[72]

This descendant was the promised Savior.[73]

Having thus concluded his solemn covenant with Abraham, God set about the work of fulfilling it, in the unfolding of the patriarch's destiny. In due time, Isaac, the predestined son, became the father of Jacob, and Jacob became the father of the twelve patriarchs from whom the Chosen People were sprung; thus, the nation of Israel came into being.

After the death of Abraham, as God had foretold, the Chosen People, compelled by famine, left Canaan and went down to Egypt where they dwelt for 430 years.[74] At first they prospered, but were ultimately reduced to slavery by the Pharaohs. Toward the end of that bitter enslavement, God raised up Moses to deliver his people from bondage, and thus began a new and highly important chapter in the history of God's People. The choice of Moses by God was an event of imponderable magnitude; it occurred toward the close of the Third Day of the Week of Salvation History.

[72] Cf. Gen. 22:16-18.
[73] Cf. Gal. 3:8-16.
[74] Gen. 15:13; Exod. 12:40.

Chapter 15

Moses, Figure of Christ

The great mission entrusted to Moses by God was to lead forth the Chosen People from the bondage of Egypt at the time preordained by him, and to lead them back to the Promised Land. In this he was a figure of Christ the Savior, whose mission it was to deliver mankind from the slavery of the Devil and lead them back to the true Promised Land of heaven. Vested by God with grace and power to accomplish his mission, he led forth the Chosen People from Egypt with great signs and wonders and, after their departure, continued to lead them through the desert for forty years until they reached the Promised Land. But Moses did not enter the land himself, being deprived of that privilege by God for his want of perfect faith; he beheld it from afar, but he died within sight of it. It was reserved to Joshua, who succeeded Moses, to lead God's people into the land. The name *Joshua* signified "Jesus" or "Savior."

The period of forty years that Israel spent in the desert after their departure from Egypt was perhaps the most important in the history of the Chosen People, for it was during that time that they were formally constituted as a nation. This occurred when God gave Moses the written Law on Mount Sinai, and once more concluded a solemn covenant with mankind in the person of the Chosen People. This covenant was sealed with the blood of sacrificed victims, which was sprinkled both on the people and on the Book of the Law which Moses had written at the command of God. The covenant was a bilateral agreement by which God chose Israel as his special possession above all the peoples of the earth, and they chose him as their God. By these solemn rites Israel was constituted a nation with its own Law and its own ritual of divine worship.

The Law of Israel was destined to exercise a profound influence on the history of Israel in future ages, as an effective instrument in welding the Chosen People into a strong and unified nation. Basically it was the Natural Law translated into the written word, with additional ordinances to cover the needs of this pilgrim people. The whole Law could be summed up in the two Great Commandments: "You shall love the Lord your God with your whole heart, and with your whole soul, and with your whole strength, and with your whole mind; and you shall love your neighbor as yourself." Ages later Jesus would say: "On these two commandments depend the whole Law and the prophets."[75]

The Law governed every aspect of Israel's life — personal, social, economic, political, and religious. It was a good moral code, yet not perfect, in that it admitted the principle of revenge. "An eye for an eye and a tooth for a tooth" was the standard norm of the Law.[76] And while commanding love of neighbor, it did not reach beyond, to admit love of enemies.[77] For the time being, however, it was sufficient for Man's needs, since he had not yet attained to a spiritual or moral stature that could accept anything higher. It would pertain to the mission of the Savior to perfect the Law in this matter.

The covenant concluded on Mount Sinai between God and his people was destined to endure until the Savior would come to

[75] Matt. 22:35-40.

[76] Cf. Exod. 21:24; Matt. 5:38.

[77] Cf. Matt. 5:43.

conclude the new and eternal covenant of redemption with mankind.[78] Having thus chosen Israel as his people, God thenceforth protected them by a special providence. During their forty years of wandering in the desert, he provided them with a mysterious bread they called *manna* to sustain them in that land unknown. But once they reached the Promised Land, the manna ceased to appear, because the people had no further need of it.

It is only when viewing the Third Day of Salvation History in retrospect that we can discern the mysterious pattern of the divine action in the world during that particular age, because in the unfolding of the destiny of the Chosen People, God was presenting to mankind a silent tableau of the whole mystery of salvation, from its opening scene to its close. The history of Israel at this time might be compared to a great drama, the four major acts of which were as follows:

• The enforced departure of the Children of Israel from the land of Canaan as a result of famine signified the casting forth of the human race from the Garden of Paradise, in the person of our first parents.

• The long exile of the Chosen People in the alien land of Egypt signified Man's abiding alienation from God after his being sent forth from Eden. The enslavement of the people by Pharaoh signified Man's enslavement by the Devil.

• Their final deliverance by Moses signified the final redemption of mankind by Jesus. Their journey under the leadership of Moses through the desert to the Promised Land symbolized the journey of the Church under the

[78] Cf. Gal. 3:13-19.

leadership of Jesus, through the desert of time to the true Promised Land of heaven.

• Their final entrance into the Promised Land under Joshua signified the final entrance of the Church into eternal life, under the leadership of Jesus, the true Savior.

From a survey of the history of Israel during this Third Day of Salvation History, we can also perceive that the Chosen People in their collective personality and destiny were a figure of the Church, for the mysterious events of this age were prophetic symbols of future mysteries in the Church of Christ.

Thus we see that the Church of the Old Covenant, founded upon the Twelve Tribes of Israel, foreshadowed the Church of the New Covenant, founded upon the Twelve Apostles. This prophetic symbolism or spiritual affinity was clearly revealed in St. John's vision of the New Jerusalem, in which he saw the Twelve Apostles of Jesus as the twelve foundations of the Holy City, while the names of the Twelve Tribes of Israel were inscribed above the twelve gates thereof.[79] The Chosen People, moreover, who were the faithful of the Old Covenant, prefigured the faithful of the New, the Christian Church.

Continuing the comparison, we see that the Law of Moses prefigured the Law of Christ. Indeed, the Law of Christ was the Law of Moses brought to perfection, as Jesus himself said: "I came not to abolish the law and the prophets but to fulfill them."[80] Like the Mosaic Law, the New Law of Christ can be summed up in the Two Great Commandments: "You shall love the Lord your God . . . and you shall love your neighbor as yourself." The Law of Moses

---

[79] Apoc. 21:12-14 (RSV = Rev. 21:12-14).
[80] Cf. Matt. 5:17.

governed the life of the Church under the Old Covenant; the Law of Christ governs the Church under the New Covenant.

As we have mentioned, the Law of Moses provided the Chosen People with their own temple and a very specialized ritual of divine worship, and both the Temple and its liturgical worship foreshadowed the Church of the New Covenant. For the Temple was a prophetic symbol of the Church of Christ, while the ceremonies of its liturgical worship foreshadowed the mysteries of the Church of the New Testament, as the author of Hebrews expressly stated: "They were shadows of the good things to come, not the very image of the things, but patterns of the true."[81]

The sacrifices of the Temple were likewise prophetic foreshadowings of the great sacrifice of redemption and would cease to have effect once the redemption had been accomplished. The angel Gabriel had signified this to the prophet Daniel when, speaking of the future sacrifice of the Redeemer, he said: . . . and after sixty-two weeks Christ shall be slain . . . and he shall confirm the covenant with many in one week; and in the half of the week the victim and the sacrifice shall fail . . ."[82] The Church observes that the angel thereby signified that all the victims and sacrifices of the Old Law would cease to be effective after the sacrifice of redemption had been accomplished, having then fulfilled their purpose.

These sacrifices were of themselves powerless to effect the redemption of mankind, as the author of Hebrews observed when he said: "They could never make the comers thereunto perfect."[83] The Sacrifice of Christ, the Redeemer, on the contrary, which they prefigured, would effect the salvation of mankind.

---

[81] Cf. Heb. 10:1; 9:24.
[82] Dan. 9:26-27.
[83] Heb. 10:1.

Reflecting upon the sacrifice of Christ in relation to the various sacrifices of the Old Law, the inspired writer continued:

> But Christ, being come a high priest of the good things to come, neither by the blood of goats or calves, but by his own blood, entered once into the holies, having obtained eternal redemption. For if the blood of goats or of oxen being sprinkled, sanctify such as are defiled, to the cleansing of the flesh, how much more shall the blood of Christ, who by the Holy Spirit offered himself unspotted to God, cleanse our conscience from dead works to serve the living God? And therefore he is the mediator of the new testament: that by means of his death, for the redemption of those transgressions which were under the former testament, they that are called may receive the promise of eternal inheritance.[84]

But while all the sacrifices of the Old Covenant foreshadowed the sacrifice of redemption, not all of them necessarily foreshadowed its exact nature. There were, however, four prophetic types during this Third Day of Salvation History that graphically foreshadowed the sacrifice of the Savior: the sacrifice of Melchisedek,[85] the sacrifice of Isaac,[86] the sacrifice of the Paschal Lamb,[87] and the incident of the bronze serpent in the desert.[88] The last three mentioned prefigured the sacrifice of Calvary.

Let us now consider these prophetic sacrifices briefly. Abraham's willingness to sacrifice his son Isaac was a prophetic image

[84] Heb. 9:11-15.
[85] Gen. 14:18-20.
[86] Gen. 22:1-13.
[87] Exod. 12.
[88] Num. 21:5-9.

of the eternal Father himself, who ages later would give his only-begotten Son as a Sacrifice for the redemption of the world. Jesus himself signified this to Nicodemus at the beginning of his public life when he said:

> God so loved the world as to give his only-begotten Son, that whosoever believes in him may not perish but may have life everlasting. For God did not send his Son into the world to condemn the world but that the world may be saved by him."[89]

Isaac, the intended victim of the sacrifice, who carried the wood of his own sacrifice to the Mount of Vision, was a graphic image of Jesus carrying the wood of his own sacrifice to the Mount of Calvary. Many scholars today are of the opinion that the Mount of Vision was actually Calvary.

The Paschal Lamb, the most solemn sacrifice of the Chosen People, was first offered to God the eternal Father, as he himself had commanded, and then was eaten as food by the people. This, too, was a graphic image of the Sacrifice of Jesus, the Lamb of God renewed in the sacrifice of the Eucharist, who, having offered himself to the Father by the hands of the priest, becomes the food of his people in Holy Communion.

The incident of the bronze serpent foreshadowed in a singular manner the nature of the Redeemer's Sacrifice. It occurred during the sojourn in the desert when the people were attacked by venomous serpents whose bite caused death. Seeing the great destruction wrought by this plague, Moses appealed to God to save the people. Forthwith, God commanded him to set up a bronze serpent in the midst of the community, promising that all who looked

---

[89] John 3:16-17.

upon it would be saved from death.[90] It was a graphic image of the Cross of Jesus, who in death was reputed as a worm and no Man and was set up as a sign of salvation for all the people.[91] Jesus declared to Nicodemus that the bronze serpent was a foreshadowing of the mystery of his death, saying: "As Moses lifted up the serpent in the desert, so must the Son of Man be lifted up, that whosoever believes in him may not perish but may have life everlasting."[92]

And as the sacrifices of the Old Law foreshadowed the great Sacrifice of the New, so the priesthood of the Old Law foreshadowed the priesthood of the New. But the priesthood of the New Law was immeasurably superior to that of the Old, being derived from Christ, the great High Priest of mankind. This was clearly shown at the dawn of the Third Day of the Salvation Week, in the mysterious incident of the blessing of Abraham by Melchisedek. This unknown personage appeared suddenly as if from nowhere on the pages of Sacred Scripture, without genealogy or ancestral record of any kind to reveal his identity. Nothing, in fact, is known of him except that he was high priest and king of Jerusalem. His name and title signified "king of justice and peace."[93]

The book of Genesis relates that on one occasion, Abraham was returning victorious after having defeated four invading alien kings, when Melchisedek went forth to meet him and blessed him, offering at the same time a sacrifice of bread and wine in thanksgiving to God; whereupon Abraham offered to Melchisedek tithes of the spoils he had taken in battle.[94]

---

[90] Num. 21:9.
[91] Cf. Ps. 21:7 (RSV = Ps. 22:6); Isa. 11:10.
[92] John 3:14-15.
[93] Heb. 7:2.
[94] Gen. 14:18-20.

Commenting upon this mysterious scene, the author of Hebrews says that here Melchisedek was a prophetic type of Christ, both in the obscure nature of his unrecorded origin and in his twofold office of king and high priest. Thus, observed the sacred writer, he was "without father, without mother, without genealogy, having neither beginning of days nor end of life, likened unto the Son of God, he continues a priest forever."[95] In this obscurity of origin he foreshadowed Christ, the High Priest and King of all mankind, whose origin, according to his divine nature, is veiled in the mystery of eternity. Of this divine origin the prophets could say: "His generation who shall declare? His going forth is from the beginning, from the days of eternity."[96]

Melchisedek in a special manner prefigured the priesthood of Christ, because David foretold that the Savior would be a priest according to the order, or, as we would say, after the manner of Melchisedek. He said, prophetically addressing the Messiah: "The Lord has sworn and he will not repent: You are a priest forever according to the order of Melchisedek."[97] Jesus himself, in one of his verbal conflicts with the authorities in Jerusalem, clearly indicated that this psalm referred to him, and questioned them about its hidden meaning.[98]

Commenting upon the priesthood of the Old Law and of the New, the author of Hebrews showed that the priesthood of Melchisedek, and therefore the priesthood of Christ, which it typified, was superior to the priesthood of Aaron. He says that Abraham, after his victory, was blessed by Melchisedek and gave him a

[95] Heb. 7:3.
[96] Cf. Isa. 53:8; Mic. 5:2.
[97] Ps. 109:4 (RSV = Ps. 110:4).
[98] Cf. Matt. 22:41-46.

portion of his spoils. Therefore, since a lesser is always blessed by a greater, it follows that Melchisedek was greater than Abraham. But in blessing Abraham, Melchisedek blessed the priesthood that would later derive from him through Levi and Aaron. Consequently, the priesthood of Melchisedek was greater than that of Aaron, as was the priesthood of Christ which that of Melchisedek typified.[99]

The priesthood of the New Covenant, as instituted by Christ, was not a continuation of the Levitical priesthood, which ministered under the Old Law; it was something entirely different, because Aaron was of the tribe of Levi, whereas Jesus, according to his human nature, was of the tribe of Judah. Jesus, moreover, by his own divine authority, instituted the priesthood that was to minister under the New Covenant, as he also instituted the Sacrifice it was to offer. And it was a priesthood according to the order (that is, manner) of Melchisedek, because the Sacrifice that the priesthood of the New Law was deputed to offer was nothing other than Jesus himself, the great Victim of redemption, present in the sacrament of the Eucharist, in his Body, Blood, Soul, and Divinity, under the appearances of bread and wine.[100]

It is only in retrospect that we can see how marvelously the sacrifice of bread and wine offered by Melchisedek foreshadowed the sacrifice of the Eucharist, which was to be offered under the New Law.

Then there was the manna, that mysterious food with which God sustained his people during the forty years of wandering in the desert.[101] Miraculously given, it became the bread of the Chosen

[99] Cf. Heb. 7:1-12.
[100] Cf. Heb. 7:13-18.
[101] Cf. Exod. 16.

People until they reached the Promised Land. It was a prophetic figure of the Eucharist, the sacrament of the Body and Blood, Soul and Divinity of Christ, which are really and truly present under the appearances of bread and wine. This is the sacrament Jesus gave to his people, the New Israel, to be their food on their pilgrimage through time to the Promised Land of heaven. He himself signified this when he said to the multitude in the desert on the day after the feeding of the five thousand with five loaves and two fishes. He said to them:

> Moses did not give you bread from heaven, but my Father gives you the true bread from heaven. For the bread of God is that which comes down from heaven and gives life to the world . . .
>
> I am the bread of life. He that comes to me shall not hunger, and he that believes in me shall never thirst . . . Your fathers did eat manna in the desert and are dead. This is the bread which comes down from heaven, that if any Man eat of it he may not die.
>
> I am the living bread which came down from heaven . . . Not as your fathers did eat manna and are dead, he that eats this bread shall live forever; the bread that I will give is my flesh for the life of the world. Except you eat the flesh of the Son of Man and drink his blood, you shall not have life in you. He that eats my flesh and drinks my blood has everlasting life; and I will raise him up on the last day.[102]

Thus, we see that the revelation of this Third Day of the Week of Salvation History showed that the promised Savior, like the Paschal Lamb that prefigured him, would be a victim of sacrifice

[102]Cf. John 6:32-59.

for his people, and afterward become their food in the sacrament of his Body and Blood. The sacrament of the Eucharist is the "manna" of the New Covenant, which sustains the Church on her pilgrimage to eternal life. Like the manna of the Old Covenant, it will cease when mankind reaches the true Promised Land of heaven, for it will no longer be needful, since Man will have come into the possession of God, the Infinite Good.

Lastly, we come to consider the old Mosaic covenant itself, which foreshadowed the New and Eternal covenant of God with mankind, in the mystery of redemption. The angel Gabriel had spoken to the prophet Daniel about this New Covenant about five centuries before the Savior actually came,[103] and the prophet Jeremiah also had much to say about it. The latter saw the New Covenant of redemption as the eternal covenant to which the Mosaic covenant looked forward. Thus he said:

> Behold the days are coming, says the Lord, when I will make a new covenant with the house of Israel and with the house of Judah; not according to the covenant which I made with their fathers on the day that I took them by the hand, to bring them out of the land of Egypt. But this shall be the covenant that I shall make with the house of Israel after those days, says the Lord: I will write my law in their hearts; and I will be their God and they shall be my people. And they shall teach no more, every Man his brother, saying, "Know the Lord," for all shall know me, from the least to the greatest. For I will forgive their iniquity, and I will remember their sin no more.[104]

---

[103]Cf. Dan. 9:23-27.
[104]Jer. 31:31-34.

Commenting upon this passage, the author of Hebrews said: "Now, in saying 'new' he made the former 'old.' And that which decays and grows old is near its end."[105]

On the night before his death, Jesus revealed that the sacrifice of redemption was the New Covenant of which Jeremiah had spoken. During the Last Supper, "he took bread and blessed and broke and gave to his disciples and said: 'Take ye and eat: This is my body, which is given for you.' And taking the chalice, he gave thanks and gave to them saying: 'Drink ye all of this. For this is my blood of the new testament, which shall be shed for many for the remission of sins."[106]

On Mount Sinai God concluded the Old Covenant with his people amid scenes of awesome splendor. There was a dark cloud, the roar of thunder, and the flashing of lightning. On Calvary he concluded the new and eternal covenant with his people amid similar scenes. There was the mysterious darkness that covered the earth from the sixth to the ninth hour, while Jesus was actually offering the sacrifice of redemption on the Cross; and the thunderous sound of the earthquake that rent the rocks and tore the Temple veil asunder, signifying, according to the author of Hebrews, that the mystery hidden from former ages was now revealed, and the gates of heaven were now reopened to mankind.[107]

In the Old Covenant, God received his people in love and friendship; in the New Covenant, he again received them definitively in the love and friendship of the great reconciliation of redemption. As the fruit of that redemption, Man recovered his primal inheritance, the gift of sanctifying grace, which would

[105]Heb. 8:13.
[106]Matt. 26:26, 27-28; Mark 14:24; Luke 22:19, 20.
[107]Cf. Heb. 9-10; John 3:13-17; Eph. 3:1-11.

enable him to enter eternal life to enjoy forever the divine society and friendship of God, in whose likeness he was made.

From these considerations it is evident how profoundly mysterious was the work of God in his preparation of the future mystery of the Church during this Third Day of the Week of Salvation History. Throughout this Day, God was working to bring to perfection his redemptive plan for mankind. On a natural plane, he brought into being the people and the nation of the Savior and presided over the unfolding of their destiny with a wonderful providence. On a supernatural plane, he caused his revelation to mankind to grow in depth and clarity, like the brightening dawn that gradually grows to the light of perfect day, or the waters in Ezekiel's vision, which grew ever deeper until they could not be forded unaided.[108] For during this epoch, he gave to mankind a prophetic view of the most profound mysteries of the future Church of Christ, those mysteries in which the finite touches upon the infinite and time mingles with eternity.

The closing period of this Third Day saw the re-entrance of the Children of Israel into the Promised Land after forty years of wandering in the desert. Having settled in, they divided the land by lot among the tribes and, for about two centuries thereafter, lived in a kind of loose federation of tribal states under the leadership of military leaders called Judges.

At the end of that time, David, who was a member of the tribe of Judah, was elected king over Israel, and this historic event brought the Third Day of the Week of Salvation History to a close.

[108]Ezek. 47:1-12.

Chapter 16

The Fourth Day: From David to Babylon

The Fourth Day of the Week of Salvation History began with the anointing of David as king over Israel about the year 1010 BC and lasted until the Babylonian Exile, which began in 587 BC. That is a period of about four centuries.

Although a member of the princely tribe of Judah, David began his life as a shepherd boy on the hillsides of Bethlehem, totally unaware of the great destiny to which he would one day be called by God. Of a naturally contemplative disposition, he was gifted with an innate genius for music and song, and all unknowingly was himself the harp of the Holy Spirit, for while tending his flocks on the hillsides, he composed under divine inspiration many beautiful hymns in praise of God. These treated of every aspect of the divine perfections, from the omnipotent power and majesty of God to the divine tenderness in receiving back an erring soul to repentance. Besides this, they contained many profound and mysterious prophecies about the Savior, who, according to the promises of God, would be a descendant of his.[109] These inspired psalms were destined to become later one of the most important and treasured possessions of the Church's liturgical patrimony under both the Old and the New Covenants.

---

[109] Ps. 109 (RSV = Ps. 110); Matt. 22:41-46; Luke 1:31-33.

David's life as a shepherd boy came to a close when the finger of God reached down and drew him forth from obscurity to make him king of the Chosen People. He was anointed by the prophet Samuel, to replace Saul, who had proved unworthy of his office, and with this event the tide of his life's destiny changed forever.

As king, David showed himself an efficient and able ruler, and under his leadership, the kingdom attained great heights of temporal glory; but his splendid achievements made him proud and ambitious and ultimately led him to moral ruin. To gratify his desire, he committed adultery and murder in order to obtain the wife of Urias, one of his most trusted officers, and he did not even repent of his deed until he was rebuked by the prophet Nathan. Touched by the prophet's rebuke, he became sincerely repentant and tried by every means in his power to make amends for his transgression.[110]

David proposed to build a temple to the Lord in Jerusalem, to replace the Tabernacle, or portable temple, that had served the Chosen People since the days of the Exodus and which at that time was set up permanently in Shiloh; but God made known to him through the prophet Nathan that this work would be accomplished not by him but by his son Solomon.[111] Nevertheless, in reward for his generous desire, God renewed his covenant with him as he had already done with Noah, Abraham, and Moses, promising that of his descendants the Savior would come.[112]

A thousand years later, the angel Gabriel, when speaking to the Virgin Mary at the time of the Incarnation, alluded to this covenant when he said, concerning the Savior who was to be born

[110] 2 Kings 11, 12 (RSV = 2 Sam. 11, 12).
[111] 2 Kings 7 (RSV = 2 Sam. 7).
[112] Cf. 1 Paralip. 17:10-22 (RSV = 1 Chron. 17:10-22).

of her: "He shall be great, and shall be called the Son of the Most High. And the Lord God shall give unto him the throne of David his father, and he shall reign in the house of Jacob forever. And of his kingdom there shall be no end."[113]

Realizing that he was not destined to build the temple himself, he nonetheless collected all the materials necessary for its construction and earnestly requested his son Solomon, who was to succeed him, to make this the first concern of his reign.[114] Meanwhile he himself did what lay in his power to enhance the splendor of the liturgical worship of the nation. To this end, he transferred the Tabernacle from Shiloh to Jerusalem and reorganized the whole ceremonial of public worship. Thus, in order to ensure the solemn and uninterrupted celebration of the liturgy, he divided the descendants of Aaron into twenty-four priestly families, assigning to each in turn its own proper time to officiate at the Temple services. He also reorganized the Levites, appointing them as porters, overseers, and choir singers at the liturgical celebrations.[115]

In every phase of his life, David was a prophetic type of Christ. In the innocence of his youth, as he tended his flocks on the hills, he prefigured Jesus, the eternal Shepherd of mankind; and even in his sinful state, he prefigured the Savior laden with the sins of the world. Having reigned as king for forty years, he died and was succeeded by his son Solomon.

Solomon was about eighteen years old when he began to rule, and like his father, he reigned as king for about forty years. He was a man of extraordinary genius, a ruler of consummate ability, an architect of the first rank, and a man of letters with a natural gift

[113]Luke 1:32-33.
[114]1 Paralip. 22:1-11 (RSV = 1 Chron. 22:1-11).
[115]1 Paralip. 23-24 (RSV = 1 Chron. 23-24).

for poetry. Endowed by God with an extraordinary gift of wisdom, he brought the kingdom to such a degree of temporal prosperity and splendor that his name and the magnificence of his rule have become proverbial among all peoples.

Commenting upon the glory of his reign, the sacred writer said:

> Now Solomon was magnified above all the kings of the earth for riches and glory; and the weight of gold that was brought to him every year was six hundred and sixty-six talents, besides the sum which the deputies of diverse nations and the merchants were accustomed to bring and all the kings of Arabia and the lords of the lands who brought gold and silver to Solomon. For the king's ships went to Tharsis with the servants of Hiram, king of Tyre, once in three years, and they brought thence gold and silver and ivory.
>
> And all the kings of the earth desired to see Solomon's face that they might hear the wisdom which God had given in his heart. And every year they brought him presents, vessels of silver and gold, and garments and armor and spices. Horses were brought to him out of Egypt and out of all countries. And Solomon had forty thousand horses in the stalls, and twelve thousand chariots and horsemen; and he placed them in the cities of the chariots and where the king was in Jerusalem. And he exercised authority over all the kings, from the river Euphrates to the land of the Philistines and to the borders of Egypt.
>
> And Solomon made a great throne of ivory and overlaid it with gold. There was not such a throne in any kingdom. And all the vessels of the king's table were of gold, for no account was made of silver in those days, and the king made stairs in the house of the Lord and in the king's house, of

thyme trees, and harps and psalteries for the singing men. Never were there seen such trees in the land of Judah. And he made silver as plentiful as stones in Jerusalem, and cedars as common as sycamores that grow in the plains.[116]

Besides all this, Solomon wrote prolifically on the loftiest subjects, in both prose and poetry. His writings, like those of his father David, contain many profound prophecies about the person and mission of Christ, and they form part of the divinely inspired Scriptures of the Church's Canon.

Solomon's greatest material achievement was the building of the Temple in Jerusalem, which followed the pattern of the old Tabernacle, as God had shown it to Moses on Mount Sinai. It became renowned in the ancient world for the magnificence of its architecture and the splendor of its liturgical ceremony.

In the spiritual sphere, Solomon was vested with a specific vocation in the Church, being like his father David, a prophetic type of Christ, both in his name, Solomon, which means "the Peaceful,"[117] and in the magnificence of his kingly rule. Indeed, it would seem as if God designedly raised him up to bring the nation of Israel to a degree of temporal splendor that would be worthy of Jesus, the Savior of mankind and "the Desired of all nations."[118] But, like King David, his father, Solomon, too, fell to great depths of moral degradation and even became an idolater; it is not known whether he repented before his death, so that he is at once one of the greatest glories and greatest tragedies of the human race. Yet, despite this, his name is linked forever with the mystery and destiny of the

[116]Cf. 2 Paralip. 9:11-31 (RSV = 2 Chron. 9:11-31).

[117]1 Paralip. 22:9 (RSV = 1 Chron. 22:9).

[118]Agg. 2:8 (RSV = Hag. 2:8).

Church. He died after forty years of impressive kingly rule and was buried in Bethlehem, the City of David.[119]

During this Fourth Day of the Week of Salvation History, while God was using David and Solomon to bring the temporal kingdom of Israel to the apex of its material splendor, he was also at work on a spiritual plane in the field of prophecy, for this was the Golden Age of prophecy in Israel. It was at this time that the Holy Spirit began to etch the features of the Promised Savior upon the soul of Israel through the ministry of his inspired prophets. Two of the four major prophets, Isaiah and Jeremiah, and most of the twelve minor prophets flourished in Israel during this Fourth Day.

It was the divinely appointed mission of the prophets to describe in marvelous detail the peerless moral beauty of the Redeemer, and to reveal in the measure preordained by God the nature and scope of his mission. They spoke of him as the Son of God and the Son of Man, the Teacher, the Shepherd, and the High Priest of mankind. They spoke of him figuratively and metaphorically as the Root, the Stem, the Branch, the Bud, the Flower, the Fruit, the Star of Jacob, the Orient Dawn, and the Sun of Justice. They spoke of him as a Man of Sorrows destined to suffer deep affliction in the fulfillment of his mission as Savior. They spoke of his ultimate triumph over death and of his final exaltation in glory at the right hand of the Father in heaven. Lastly, they revealed him as being invested by the Father with the universal kingship of all ages and nations.[120]

As a result of this prophetic grace in Israel, the Promised Savior became the theme of Israel's song, and so perfectly did the

---

[119]2 Paralip. 9:31 (RSV = 2 Chron. 9:31).
[120]Dan. 7:9-14.

prophets portray him that when he came, the nation could recognize him from this prophetic likeness.

After the death of Solomon, the temporal kingdom that he and his father David had brought to such great heights of material prosperity and glory began to show signs of disintegration. Ten of the twelve tribes revolted from Roboam, the son and successor of Solomon, because of his tyranny, and founded an independent kingdom in the north, which they called the kingdom of Israel; the two remaining tribes in the south, Judah and Benjamin, founded the rival kingdom of Judah. For two and a half centuries after the death of Solomon, these two kingdoms were torn by internal jealousy and strife. Then, in 722 BC, the great Assyrian empire swept down from the north and carried away the Ten Tribes — the kingdom of Israel — into captivity from which they never returned.

After the deportation, the Assyrians placed settlers of their own in the northern kingdom of Israel, to replace the native population. These intermarried with the remnant of the Israelites who were left behind, and thus the northern kingdom became the home of a new race of mixed origins, who were later known as the Samaritans. This new race was despised by the southern kingdom of Judah, which refused to regard them as true Israelites, and so a mutual hostility developed between the two peoples. In time, this antagonism became very bitter and survived until the Gospel times.[121]

Almost a century and a half after the deportation of the Ten Tribes, Nebuchadnezzar, king of Babylon, carried away the remaining two tribes of the southern kingdom of Judah, and they remained in exile in Babylon for seventy years. This exile, which

---

[121]Cf. John 4.

brought the Fourth Day of the Week of Salvation History to a close, began in the year 587 BC and is known as the Babylonian Captivity.[122]

At first sight, it might seem strange that God should have allowed the disintegration of the temporal kingdom that he himself had called into being, but on deeper reflection we can see that it was willed for a specific purpose. The disintegration of the temporal kingdom was like the mystery of the ripe fruit that falls to the ground and dies, only to spring up again in an immeasurably greater harvest. This was all a part of God's preparation of Israel for the coming of the Savior. For the temporal kingdom of Israel was in reality a symbol of the new and spiritual kingdom of the New Israel, which would one day spring from it as from a holy root.[123] This New Israel, which the Old foreshadowed, was the Church of Christ, which would one day spread far beyond the geographical boundaries of the temporal kingdom, to envelop all ages and nations within its mystery.[124]

[122]Cf. Jer. 52.

[123]Luke 1:31-33; Gal. 2:13-29, 4:22-31.

[124]Dan. 2:44, 7:9-14; Matt. 28:18-21.

Chapter 17

The Fifth Day: From Babylon to Christ

The Fifth Day of the Salvation Week began with the Babylonian Captivity in 587 BC and lasted until the coming of Christ — that is, a period of almost six centuries. The Babylonian Captivity was permitted by God as a punishment for the sins of the Chosen People, particularly that of idolatry, and it was the final preparation of his people for the coming of the Savior.

During this Day, God was at work on both a natural and a supernatural plane, bringing to completion his age-long preparation for the coming of Christ. At this time he might be compared to a great composer, drawing together into final harmony the diverse elements of human history in order to perfect the Great Symphony of the Ages. On a supernatural plane, it was during this epoch that he made some of his most important revelations to the prophets in regard to the exact time of the Savior's coming, the nature of the Savior's Redemptive Sacrifice, the continuation of that sacrifice under the New Covenant, and the nature of the Savior's kingdom.

On a natural plane, he began to draw together the various strands of political events in the international arena, to make ready the stage of history for the entrance of his only-begotten Son into the world. For during this Day, the great Gentile powers were providentially drawn into the orbit of Israel's history. Chief among these were the Persian, Greek, and Roman empires, all of which were destined by God to play a highly important role in the mystery of salvation. At this time also, many of the great figures who were destined to play a key role in the mystery of Christ moved into place on the stage of history, as the Great Drama of redemption mounted toward its climax. It was perhaps for this reason that St. Paul referred to this age as "the fullness of time."[125]

As we have previously observed, this great Fifth Day dawned when Nebuchadnezzar, king of Babylon, swept down with his armies and devastated the kingdom of Judah (587 BC); he destroyed the city of Jerusalem and burned the beautiful Temple of Solomon, then carried away almost the entire population of the kingdom into captivity in Babylon. There the Chosen People remained for seventy years to make reparation for their age-long infidelity to God, while their own land mourned in solitude, and Jerusalem lay a desolate waste. The magnitude of that desolation was graphically described by the prophet Jeremiah in his "Lamentations" over the Holy City, in which he said:

> Lo, how the city sits solitary, that was full of people! How is the mistress of the Gentiles become a widow: the princes of the provinces made tributary! Weeping she has wept in the night and her tears are on her cheeks. There is none to comfort her among all of them that were dear to her. All her friends have despised her and are become her enemies. Judah has removed her dwelling place, because of the greatness of her bondage; she has dwelt among the nations and found no rest . . . The ways of Sion mourn because there are none that come to the solemn feasts. All her gates are broken down, her priests sigh, her virgins are in affliction, and

[125]Gal. 4:4.

she is oppressed with bitterness. Her adversaries are become her lords, her enemies are enriched . . . her children are led into captivity before the face of the oppressor, and from the daughter of Sion all her beauty is departed . . . To what shall I compare you or to what shall I liken you . . . that I may comfort you, O virgin daughter of Sion? For great as the sea is your destruction. Who shall heal you?[126]

If the desolation of the land and of the Holy City was great, greater still was that of the exiles themselves. The depths of their desolation was very poignantly described in one of Israel's most beautiful psalms, which says: "By the rivers of Babylon, there we sat and wept, remembering Sion. Upon the willows of that land we hung up our harps. There our captors asked songs of us, and our tormentors mirth: sing to us they said, the songs of Sion. Oh, how could we sing a song of the Lord in an alien land?"[127] But this chastisement, bitter though it was, was willed by God for his people's healing, not for their destruction, and it is noteworthy that after their return from exile, they never again were guilty of idolatry.

In exile the Chosen People suffered numerous hardships, including the loneliness of exile itself, but God did not abandon them in their distress; rather, at this very time he raised up some of Israel's greatest prophets to console and encourage them. Among these were Ezekiel and Daniel. To Ezekiel God made known many things about the future destiny of the Church, particularly in regard to the overflowing grace of redemption, in the vision of the Holy Waters.[128] To Daniel he revealed the time of the Savior's coming.

[126]Lam. 1:1-6; 2:13.
[127]Ps. 136:1-4 (RSV = Ps. 137:1-3).
[128]Cf. Ezek. 47.

In answer to Daniel's prayer for the restoration of the Holy City and the nation of Israel, God made known to him through the ministry of the angel Gabriel, the time of the Savior's coming, and something of the nature of the great restoration or redemption to be effected by him. This revelation is usually referred to as the prophecy of the seventy weeks.

Speaking of the time of the Savior's coming and of the redemption he would accomplish, the angel said:

> Seventy weeks are determined for your people and for your holy city that transgression may be finished and sin may have an end, and iniquity may be abolished and everlasting justice may be brought, and vision and prophecy may be fulfilled, and the Saint of Saints may be anointed.
>
> Know therefore and take notice, that from the going forth of the word to build up Jerusalem again, until Christ the prince, there shall be seven weeks and sixty-two weeks. And after sixty-two weeks Christ shall be slain. And the people that shall deny him shall not be his. And a people with their leader shall come and shall destroy the city and the sanctuary; and the end thereof shall be waste, and after the end of the war, the appointed desolation.
>
> And he [Christ] shall confirm the covenant with many in one week, and in the half of the week the victim and the sacrifice shall fail . . . and the desolation shall continue even to the consummation and to the end.[129]

Interpreting this prophecy, the Church says that the seventy weeks were not intended to be a mathematical reckoning of time, since none of the divine works can be so reckoned. Rather, the

---

[129]Cf. Dan. 9:24-27.

The Fifth Day: From Babylon to Christ

prophecy was intended to give a broad outline of the disposition of Israel's history from the time of the exile to the coming of the Savior. Thus, a "week," as used by the angel, signified a period of seven years, not seven days. Seventy weeks, therefore, would be about 490 years, or about five centuries — approximately the length of time that elapsed between the Babylonian Exile and the birth of Christ (587 BC-6 BC). It is possible, therefore, to discern in the pattern of the seventy weeks a certain resemblance or affinity to the actual historical events of Israel's history during that period, as we shall see.

When speaking to Daniel, the angel Gabriel divided the entire seventy-week period into three parts: 1) a period of seven weeks, followed by 2) a period of sixty-two weeks, and concluding with 3) a final period of one week — the seventieth week.

There are divergent opinions among exegetes as to what these separate periods signify. Some think that the first period of seven weeks — that is, forty-nine years — might have signified the time that elapsed between the deportation of the Chosen People to Babylon in 587 BC and the edict of Cyrus, king of Persia, in 538 BC, permitting the exiles to return to their homeland.

The second period, of sixty-two weeks, about 434 years — roughly four centuries — might have signified the long period of rebuilding and reorganizing the nation, which followed upon the return of the exiles.

The final period is that of the seventieth week and might have signified the actual "Day of redemption" — that is, the period from the Baptism of Christ to the destruction of Jerusalem in the year AD 70.

Thus, we see that the first two periods taken together — that is, the seven weeks and the sixty-two weeks — comprise sixty-nine out of the seventy weeks. This period covers the entire history of Israel from the deportation of the Chosen People to Babylon, until the coming of Christ.

The important events of this age included the rebuilding of the Temple of Jerusalem at the end of the exile, the subsequent rebuilding of the city of Jerusalem by Nehemiah, and the reorganization of national life according to the Mosaic Law by Ezra the Scribe.

The seventieth week saw the actual accomplishment of the redemption by Christ and the first years of the growth of the Christian Church. The great events of this week, therefore, were the baptism and public life of Christ, his death on Calvary, his Resurrection and Ascension, and the Descent of the Holy Spirit on the Church at Pentecost. It witnessed also the growth and development of the Church, from Pentecost to the destruction of Jerusalem by the Roman general Titus in the year AD 70.

We can see from this that the final phases of Israel's history prior to the coming of Christ were clearly traced by the angel Gabriel, as a prophetic guide for those who had eyes to see, and time itself would reveal how perfectly this prophecy of the seventy weeks would be fulfilled.

Another important revelation of this Fifth Day was that given by God to Nebuchadnezzar, king of Babylon, concerning the nature of the Church of Christ. This revelation was interpreted by the prophet Daniel. The king's vision was as follows: he beheld a statue of great height that was made, from head to foot, respectively, of gold, silver, bronze, iron, and clay. Next, a stone was hewn from a mountain without the agency of human hands; it rolled down the mountain, struck the statue, and broke it into pieces. Whereupon the stone itself became a great mountain that filled the whole earth.[130]

---

[130]Dan. 2:29-35.

Interpreting the king's dream, Daniel said that the statue signified the great empires of antiquity, which, in the course of ages, would spring up, attain to great heights of glory, but would then ultimately be absorbed by the kingdom of God. He said: "In the days of those kingdoms, the God of heaven will set up a kingdom that will never be destroyed, and his kingdom shall not be delivered to another people, and it shall consume all these kingdoms, and itself stand forever."[131] This kingdom of the God of heaven to which Daniel referred was none other than the Church of Christ, the new and spiritual Israel that would embrace all ages and nations within its mystery.

The revelation of this Fifth Day was God's final word to mankind, until he sent his Son; but even while he was at work on a supernatural plane, he was also at work on a natural plane, disposing all events and circumstances in the temporal order, to bring to perfection his plan of redemption for mankind. Indeed, the divine activity in regard to the temporal destiny of Israel at this time was most mysterious and profound.

From a human point of view, it was a dark hour for Israel when the domination of foreign aggressors seemed to destroy all hope of survival, and the tyranny of brutal persecution threatened to destroy the nation from the face of the earth. Yet God was using these very persecutors to play a role in the mystery of the Church, whose profound and far-reaching influence would be beyond all reckoning. A survey of Israel's temporal destiny at that time will make this clear and show at once the wonderful providence with which God watched over his people, and the marvelous manner in which he brought his plan of redemption to perfection.

---

[131]Dan. 2:44.

Chapter 18

The Rise of Greece and Rome

For fifty years after the deportation to Babylon, the fortunes of the Chosen People remained unchanged, until Babylon itself fell before the rising power of Persia. With this event, Israel had a new overlord in the Persian conqueror. By a providential design of God, the Chosen People found favor with their new masters, and in 538 BC, the Persian king Cyrus the Great issued a decree permitting them to return to their own land. He permitted Zorobabel, a prince of Judah to return and rebuild the Temple in Jerusalem, and that was the first step toward the rebuilding of the nation.

The return from the exile, however, was at first slow and halting, and it was only about twenty years later that the full tide of return got well underway: that was seventy years after the great deportation. For two centuries more, Israel remained subject to the Persian empire, until Persia itself fell before the rising power of Greece. Then once again she changed her master.

Alexander the Great, founder of the Greek empire, conquered the Persians in the year 331 BC and thus became the new master of the Chosen People. It was at this predestined hour that the destiny of Israel became linked with the Greek civilization, which was destined to play such an important part in the mystery of salvation. Because of the nature of this mission, it might be worthwhile to consider briefly the history and culture of Greece.

The Mystery and Destiny of the Church

About 1000 BC, Greece was the first European country to become civilized, originally borrowing its civilization from ancient Babylon. Soon, however, it outstripped its ancient master and became itself the most excellent of all ancient cultures. Greece had been civilized for about seven centuries when Alexander the Great rose like a meteor upon its horizon. He dreamed of world conquest and founded the Greek empire, which stretched from Egypt to India in the east, and westward to include all the countries of the Mediterranean shoreline. This vast empire welded together in a single culture all the various races and nations it conquered, and in this way, the Greek language became the common tongue of the educated classes everywhere, while Greek manners and ideas pervaded the society of the whole civilized world.

This superb culture was to provide the language in which the message of the gospel was first preached to the Gentile world. The Hebrew Scriptures were translated into Greek about three centuries before Christ, by Jewish scholars at Alexandria. This translation was called the *Septuagint* and was used by the Evangelists in the Gospels and by St. Paul in his letters, as well as by other writers of the New Testament. Three of the four Gospels were written in Greek, while St. Matthew's, which was originally written in Aramaic, was translated into Greek less than twenty years after it was written.

The Greek language with its delicate nuances of expression was admirably suitable for the elucidation of the finer points of Christian theology and proved to be an apt instrument for furthering the development and authentic explanation of the Christian message. This was the service preordained by God, to be rendered by the Greek culture in the mystery of salvation.

About eight years after his conquest of Persia, Alexander died (323 BC), leaving his empire to four of his generals, who later founded independent dynasties of their own. Two of these dynasties, those of Egypt and Syria, later subjugated Israel during the two centuries that followed, and thus the country remained under the influence of Greek culture until the Roman conquest of Palestine by Pompey in the year 63 BC, roughly half a century before the coming of Christ.

Toward the end of the Greek period, during the century that preceded the Roman conquest, the great Maccabean dynasty arose in Israel to resist the tyranny and aggression of the Syrian kings. It had flourished for almost a century, but had begun to decline by the time of the Roman conquest, and shortly thereafter faded completely from the scene. During the rule of the Maccabean dynasty, however, Israel enjoyed a good measure of peace and prosperity, with the added blessing of freedom from foreign aggression.

Then came the moment of destiny, when, by a mysterious dispensation of divine providence, the great Roman empire was drawn into the orbit of Israel's history. Like that of Greece, the Roman civilization was destined by God to play a role of imponderable magnitude in the mystery of salvation. Originally borrowing its culture from Greece, it ultimately rivaled it in splendor. For about three centuries before the birth of Christ, the rhythmic footfall of its marching armies brought the benefits and refining influence of Roman law and culture to every corner of the civilized world. And thus, like the Greek empire before it, this superb civilization once again welded together into one political unit a whole array of diverse nations and cultures, which before had known only the chaotic confusion of barbarism.

In the year 63 BC, Pompey captured Palestine, and thus, Israel became part of the Roman empire. Thirty-five years later, Octavian became the first emperor of Rome, receiving the title of Caesar

Augustus in the year 27BC. This was the ruler who was preordained by God to issue the decree of enrollment "for the whole world," which brought Mary and Joseph to Bethlehem for the birth of Christ.

In due time, every facet of Roman civilization rendered its predestined measure of service to God in the mystery of salvation. The roads of the empire carried the message of the gospel to the ends of the civilized world. Its palaces and public buildings became the first Christian churches, while its language ultimately supplanted Greek as the official language of the Church in the West. Its citizens from all ranks of society were among the most illustrious of the Church's martyrs, while Rome itself became the Eternal City of the Church of the New Covenant. There the holy apostles Peter and Paul sealed the testimony of their Faith by martyrdom, thus making the once-pagan city the citadel of the Christian Faith from which the light of the gospel would radiate to the ends of the earth.

In rendering its appointed measure of service, Rome was aided by another dynasty that was destined by God to play a singular role in the mystery of salvation, and more particularly in the actual life of the Savior. This was the Herodian dynasty, whose founder and greatest figure was Herod the Great. The Herods came from a princely family of Idumaea, that wild and mountainous region south of the province of Judea. The Idumaeans were Edomites — that is, descendants of Esau, the brother of Jacob, who had settled originally in the region southeast of the Dead Sea. In the course of the ages, however, they were driven eastward by the powerful Nabatean Arab tribes until they finally settled in the region to which they gave their name. They were, therefore, racially akin to the Chosen People.

Herod the Great, the founder of the Herodian dynasty, was the son of Antipater, a powerful Idumaean prince and ally of Rome. In the year 40 BC, Rome allowed Herod to assume the title of king, and with that event the foundation stone of the Herodian dynasty was laid. It flourished for about a century and a half (40 BC-AD 93), yet it was never accepted by the Jewish people, first because of racial animosity, and secondly because they looked upon the Herods as usurpers and devotees of Rome.

Since Israel was a unit of the Roman Empire during the entire period of the dynasty, the rule of the Herods was always subject to the will and sanction of Rome, and although they proved themselves efficient administrators, they were in reality no more than vice-regents of their imperial masters, despite the fact that some members of the dynasty actually held the title of king.

Viewed in retrospect, it would seem as though God designedly brought this dynasty into being, to minister to the mystery of his Son. Thus, we see that Herod the Great, its founder, received the title of king from Rome only a little over thirty years before the birth of Christ, while the last member of the dynasty, King Herod Agrippa II, a great grandson of Herod the Great, died about the same time as St. John the Apostle, in the year AD 93. Thus, the history of the dynasty runs parallel to the life of Christ and to the first period of the Christian Church. Having fulfilled its divinely appointed role in the mystery of salvation, it, too, like many other temporal powers, bowed off the stage of history and vanished forever. Its role, however, was a very important one, and in a sense unique.

We see, for instance, that it was during the reign of Herod the Great, the founder of the dynasty, that Jesus was born. It was Herod who received the Magi in Jerusalem and subsequently ordered the massacre of the children in Bethlehem, in the hope of including Jesus among his victims. After his death in 4 BC, his kingdom was divided among three of his sons, Archelaus, Herod

Antipas, and Philip. Each of these sons was destined likewise to play an important role in the life of Christ.

Archelaus succeeded his father as ruler of Judea, and it was due to his tyrannical rule that Joseph, upon his return from Egypt, decided to return to Nazareth in Galilee rather than settle in Bethlehem of Judah. After ten years of misrule, Archelaus was deposed by Rome and sent into exile in Gaul. His territory was then administered by a Roman procurator, or governor. The other two brothers, Herod Antipas and Philip, were left unmolested in their territories at this time. This political arrangement of the nation remained unchanged during the entire lifetime of Jesus — that is, from about his twelfth year until his death on Calvary, about the year AD 30.

From the deposition of Archelaus in AD 6 until the Fall of Jerusalem in AD 70, the Roman governors ruled the province of Judea, and sometimes as the need arose, other sections of the country as well. There was only one brief interval during that period when the whole country was ruled by a grandson of Herod the Great, by the will and sanction of Rome. This was King Herod Agrippa I, who ruled from AD 39-44. Between the years AD 6 and AD 70, there were fourteen Roman governors of Judea. Pontius Pilate, the fifth governor, was the one who condemned Jesus to death.

Herod Antipas, the second heir of Herod the Great, became ruler of Galilee on the death of his father, receiving the title of Tetrarch from Rome. He was, therefore, the immediate temporal overlord of the Holy Family at Nazareth during the entire period of the hidden life of Jesus, after his return from Egypt. Herod Antipas continued as ruler of Galilee for about nine years after the Crucifixion, until he was deposed by Rome in AD 39 and sent into exile in Gaul, where Archelaus had preceded him more than thirty years before. There he died in obscurity.

Herod had married Herodias, the wife of Philip, his brother; this was not Philip the Tetrarch but another half-brother of the same name. He married her sometime before AD 28, and it was this event which ultimately led to the death of John the Baptist. This Herod was also the one before whom Jesus stood on trial for a brief period during his Passion. He was sent to him by Pilate, who thus hoped to extricate himself from the responsibility of the case, because Jesus, being a Galilean, was legally Herod's subject. But Herod saw through his motives and declined to judge the case and sent Jesus back to him. Yet because of this brief meeting, his name is forever linked with the mystery of the Passion of Christ.

Philip the Tetrarch, the third heir of Herod the Great, ruled the northeastern region of the country and there built his residential city, which he named Caesarea in honor of the emperor Augustus, adding his own name to distinguish it from the city of Caesarea on the Mediterranean coastline, built by his father, Herod the Great, also in honor of Augustus. Philip's city was therefore known as Caesarea Philippi. It was in the vicinity of this city that Peter proclaimed Jesus, "Christ, the Son of the living God" and received from him in return for this wonderful profession of faith, the promise that upon him, as upon a rock, he would build his Church and would bestow upon him "the keys of the kingdom of heaven."[132] This signified the office of supreme authority in the Church. Thus, by reason of this incident, the foundation of the Church of Christ is forever linked with the memory of Philip the Tetrarch.

From the foregoing considerations, we can see that the Fifth Day of the Week of Salvation History was a very important epoch in the history and mystery of the Church, one whose every activity

---

[132]Cf. Matt. 16:13-19.

was to have profound and far-reaching implications for the destiny of the Church in future ages. And it was then, at that predestined hour when all things were in readiness, and "the fullness of time had come,[133] that God sent his Son.

[133]Gal. 4:4.

Part 4

The Sixth Day:
The Age of the Church

Chapter 19

Jesus Our Savior

Any survey of universal history reveals that the great cosmic event around which the mystery of the human destiny revolves was the entrance of Christ, the Promised Savior, into the orbit of human history as God made Man. His coming was not something that took the world by surprise and found mankind totally unprepared, but something, rather, for which God had been preparing Man since the very opening chapter of the human story. It was the culmination of a divine work of ages, the focal point of human history and the coordinating element in time, for it is only in the light of his presence that time reveals that harmony of design which is characteristic of all the works of God.

He first appeared, as we have seen, in the very opening scene of the human drama, when God promised a Redeemer to our first parents, although his identity was not then revealed, and ever since that primal promise, mankind had been awaiting him as its Savior. The prophets had called him the "Desired of All Nations,"[134] for his salvation was to be for all men.

In regard to the unfolding of the divine plan of salvation, the time of his coming might be compared to the summertime, when the grain that has been planted in the spring begins to turn to gold, and all nature is clad in the full richness of its beauty in the

[134]Cf. Gen. 49:10; Agg. 2:8 (RSV = Hag. 2:8).

verdant bloom of plant and flower. In the spiritual order, it was the summertime of the Salvation Year when God, who had been at work in the field of the Church since the springtime of the world, was about to bring his plan of salvation to perfection by sending his Son into the world to perfect his work.[135]

As far as modern scholarship can determine, the date of his coming was the year 6 BC of the Christian calendar. This apparent contradiction, which says that Jesus was born in the year 6 before the birth of Christ, is only a mathematical accommodation. It is simply an arrangement to correct an error in the Christian calendar which was drawn up by Denis Exiguus, a monk of Rome, about the year AD 520. In compiling the calendar, Denis had assigned AD 1 as the year of the birth of Christ. All previous events were classified as BC, "before Christ"; all subsequent events were classified as AD, *anno Domini,* "in the year of the Lord." Later it was discovered that Denis had slightly miscalculated the date of our Lord's birth, for he was actually born about six years previous to that time. To correct the error, therefore, without having to rearrange the whole calendar, which was based on the pivotal date of AD 1, it was decided to leave it as it was, but to move the date of the birth of Christ back to 6 BC, which was its correct placement in time, and so, by this historic accommodation, we say that Jesus was born in the year 6 BC.

His entrance into the world marked the dawning of the Sixth Day of the Week of Salvation History, the opening of the great seventieth week of Daniel's prophecy.[136] Although, as we have said, Man had awaited his coming since the very dawn of the human day, it was only when he came that he discovered who the

[135]Cf. John 4:34.
[136]Dan. 9:24-27.

Savior really was, the only-begotten Son of the eternal Father, who became Man, so that, as Man, he might effect the redemption of mankind.

Being God, he could have chosen to enter the world in any manner he wished; he could have come as a conquering hero in the full glory of manhood or appeared as an unknown prophet to announce the day of salvation. But instead, he chose to enter life as all men do: by way of birth, although the mode of his generation was not according to the ordinary human law; rather, he took a human nature by a direct act of the creative power of God, which the Gospel expresses by saying that he took flesh of the Virgin Mary by the overshadowing power of the Holy Spirit.[137] This cosmic event by which the Son of God, the Eternal Word of the Father, became Man by uniting a human nature to his own divine nature is called by the Church the mystery of the Incarnation; it is one of the great fundamental mysteries of the Christian Faith.

Describing this cosmic event, St. Luke said that in the sixth month after the angel had foretold the birth of John the Baptist to Zachariah,

> the angel Gabriel was sent from God into a city of Galilee called Nazareth, to a virgin espoused to a man whose name was Joseph, of the house of David, and the virgin's name was Mary. And the angel being come in said to her: "Hail, full of grace, the Lord is with you, blessed are you among women." Who, having heard, was troubled at his saying, and thought with herself what manner of salutation this should be. But the angel said to her: "Fear not, Mary, for you have found grace with God."

---

[137]Luke 1:26-38.

"Behold, you shall conceive in your womb and shall bring forth a son, and you shall call his name Jesus. He shall be great and shall be called the Son of the Most High. And the Lord God shall give unto him the throne of David his father; and he shall reign in the house of Jacob forever. And of his kingdom there shall be no end." And Mary said to the angel: "How shall this be done, because I know not man"? And the angel answering said to her: "The Holy Spirit shall come upon you and the power of the Most High shall overshadow you, and therefore also, the Holy One which shall be born of you shall be called the Son of God . . . Because no word shall be impossible with God." And Mary said: "Behold the handmaid of the Lord, be it done to me according to your word." And the angel departed from her.[138]

Reflecting upon this supremely important revelation of Sacred Scripture, the Church says that at the moment of Mary's consent, God the Son, the Second Divine Person of the Blessed Trinity, became Man within her womb, and the mystery of the Incarnation, or the taking of a human nature, became a reality of history. St. John best expressed what this mystery meant in essence when he said: "And the Word was made flesh and dwelt among us; and we saw his glory, the glory as of the only begotten of the Father, full of grace and truth."[139]

We could say that in this mystery the eternal Son of God, the Eternal Word,[140] united a human nature to his own divine nature

---

[138]Luke 1:26-38.

[139]John 1:14.

[140]For the Church's basic teaching on the mystery of the Incarnation, see *Baltimore Catechism*, no. 3, 35 ff.; *Catechism Notes* (Dublin: The Anthonian Press, 1960), 3 ff. For an

as perfectly, for example, as the soul and body are united in any individual to make but one person; and this union of the two natures in Christ, the human and the divine natures, would last forever.

After the Incarnation, the Son of God would also be, and continue to be for all eternity, the Son of Man — that is, he was henceforth true God and true Man. The union of these two distinct natures in one person underlies the mystery of Christ; it is called by the Church the Hypostatic Union, which means the union that "stands beneath" (hypostatic) the mystery of Christ. By reason of this union, for example, the Church says that when Jesus said to the crowds on the shore: "I say to you," it was God who was speaking, but when he sat weary at Jacob's Well, it was Man who was weary.

The apostle John, in the very first chapter of his Gospel, touches upon the very essence of his divine nature when he says of him: "In the beginning was the Word, and the Word was with God, and the Word was God. All things were made by him: and without him was made nothing that was made."[141] In this passage, the apostle is speaking of the divine origin and nature of Christ prior to the Incarnation. He says that "in the beginning" — that is, beyond the frontiers of time, so to speak, in the limitless and timeless ages of eternity — Christ existed as the Word of the Father — the perfect expression of the Father's nature. As a word is the expression of one's thought, so the Son is, from eternity, the perfect expression of the Father's being; to use the modern translation of the Church's teaching: the Son is "one in being with the Father," or "consubstantial" with the Father, meaning of one

in-depth study, see *Catechism of the Catholic Church* (CCC), 115 ff.; *Summa Theologica*, II, Q. 1 ff.

[141]John 1:1-3.

substance with the Father (Nicene Creed). Because he is the Word or expression of the Father's perfection, he is by that very fact equal to the Father, for he is begotten of the Father and shares his very nature as an earthly son shares the nature of his father.

Both the Old and the New Testaments bear witness to this natural sonship of Christ, the Word of God made flesh. Thus, the book of Wisdom prophetically said of him that he was "the brightness of eternal light, the unspotted mirror of God's majesty, and the image of his goodness."[142] The author of Hebrews in the New Testament corroborates this testimony by saying that he is "the brightness of the Father's glory and the figure of his substance," or, as another translation has it, "He is the perfect copy of his nature."[143]

St. Paul was even more detailed in his exposition of the divine nature of Christ when he said of him: "He is the image of the invisible God, the firstborn [i.e., the most excellent] of all creatures. For in him were all things created in heaven and on earth, visible and invisible, whether thrones or dominations or principalities or powers. All things were created by him and in him. And he is before all, and by him all things consist. And he is the head of the body, the Church: who is the beginning, the firstborn from the dead, that in all things he may hold the primacy, because in him it has pleased the Father that all fullness should dwell.[144]

Then, developing his thought on what the mystery of the Incarnation involved, he said in his letter to the Philippians: "Being in the form of God, he did not think it robbery to be equal with God, but emptied himself, taking the form of a servant, being made in

---

[142]Wisd. 7:26.
[143]Heb. 1:1-3 (Jerusalem Bible).
[144]Col. 1:15-19.

the likeness of men and in habit found as a man . . ."[145] By the Incarnation he came to cast his lot with Man and to be identified with Man in all things save sin.[146] Therefore, following the normal course of nature, his birth took place nine months later in Bethlehem of Judah.

His coming changed the face of time and altered the tide of human history, and even to this day, his mystery exerts a profound and imponderable influence on every age and civilization. For his salvation and his gospel are for all: they appeal to the heart of Man, to that nature which molds every culture and civilization, while itself remaining unchanged. Since he came, the world can never be the same, for his claims upon Man are such as no other would ever have dared to make, and he supported these claims by works such as no other man had ever done or will ever do again. His doctrine is incomparably superior to any earthly philosophy, and he alone could say in perfect truth: "I have come that men may have life and may have it more abundantly."[147] No earthly philosophy or religious cult can give the fullness of meaning to life that the gospel of Jesus gives. No other way of life can give that sense of harmony and peace or that fullness of happiness to Man that Jesus' gospel provides.

Since he has spoken, the life of Man can never be the same, for, as the author of Hebrews says: "His word is living and active, more piercing than a two-edged sword."[148] It speaks to the very depths of Man's nature and affects the inmost thoughts of his heart. He is the supreme judge of every soul, from whom nothing can be

[145]Phil. 2:6-7.
[146]Heb. 4:15.
[147]John 10:10.
[148]Heb. 4:12.

hidden, and to him every individual must ultimately render an account of his life. One has only to scan the panorama of universal history to realize the truth of these things, and as St. John observed: "If we accept the testimony of men, the testimony of God is greater; and this is the testimony of God which he has testified in evidence for his Son."[149]

Those who receive him find the key to life, for he alone can teach men life's true meaning and dignity, as he said to Pilate: "For this was I born and for this I came into the world: that I should give testimony to the truth. Everyone who is of the truth listens to my voice."[150] Before laying down his life for the redemption of mankind, he founded his Church upon the Apostles, with Peter as their head, and before his Ascension, he commissioned them to go forth and preach his gospel of salvation to all men: "Going, therefore, teach all nations, baptizing them in the name of the Father and of the Son and of the Holy Spirit, teaching them to observe all things whatsoever I have commanded you. And behold, I am with you all days, even to the consummation of the world."[151]

His Church is the great preceptor of men, the city on the mountain, "the pillar and the ground of the truth."[152] The impress of genuine truth is manifest on every page of the Gospel and appeals to the very essence of Man's nature, because, being made in the likeness of God, Man loves essentially what is good, and when he beholds what is truly good, he reaches out to embrace it. That explains why Jesus' gospel, which, in so many things, runs contrary to Man's lower nature, has yet conquered the world.

[149] 1 John 5:9.
[150] John 18:37.
[151] Matt. 28:19-20.
[152] Cf. Matt. 5:14; 1 Tim. 3:15.

His gospel is suited to every age in time, to every culture and civilization and to every condition of life, because the truths it teaches are eternal and unchangeable, and therefore fill the deepest needs of Man's changeless nature. This explains, likewise, the universal appeal of Jesus to every age. He receives every soul who accepts him and sets the compass of its life to God, who is the source and end of Man's being. He is the safe anchor of every human life that is set adrift on the turbulent ocean of this world; following him, the soul will come by a swift and sure course to the goal of eternal life.

This is the portrait of Jesus as etched by the Holy Spirit on the pages of the Gospels. It reveals him as the Shepherd, Teacher, and Savior of mankind, the Son of the living God who was also the Son of Man, one person uniting a divine and a human nature in himself. The living voice that speaks to all the ages through the Gospels is the same that first spoke over the great void saying: "Let it be!" — and creation came to be. Looking upon the face of Jesus as it is revealed in the Gospels is like looking into the depths of eternity, and listening to his voice. Man at last learns the answer to the deepest yearnings of the human heart. Jesus is at once the Source and the End of life, the path which leads to life, and that life itself, which is the goal of Man's eternal quest.

The Sixth Day of the Week of Salvation, the great Day of redemption, which was ushered in by his coming, will, as we have said, know no sunset; rather, its ultimate perspectives will be mingled with the mystery of eternity. For Christ's Second Coming at the end of time will usher in the Seventh and last Day of the Salvation Week, the Eternal Sabbath rest.[153] It will signal the translation of the Church from earth to heaven, when Jesus will lead

[153]Heb. 3-4.

redeemed mankind to the fountains of the waters of life[154] and to the unveiled vision of God's glory in the home of eternal life.

So we see that Jesus is like a divine lodestar placed by the Father at the very heart of creation to bring all things together into one harmonious design of God's eternal glory.

---

[154] Apoc. 7:17 (RSV = Rev. 7:17).

Chapter 20

Christ Institutes His Church

It pertained to the mission of Christ as Savior of mankind to bring the mystery of the Church to its perfection, for he was to be the Savior of all men, not just the Savior of Israel. It was necessary, therefore, to gather into one family the members of the human race, who, throughout the long ages since the Fall, had become alienated from one another by the ravages of time and sin.

The high priest Caiphas inadvertently touched upon this aspect of the Church in his speech to the council a short time before the death of Jesus. He said: "You know nothing; neither do you consider that it is expedient for you that one man should die for the people so that the whole nation may not perish." And St. John remarked: "Now this he said not of himself, but being the high priest of that year, he prophesied that Jesus should die for the nation. And not only for the nation, but to gather together in one the children of God that were dispersed."[155]

Jesus himself gave us a deep insight into the nature of his Church when he said: "I am the good shepherd; and I know mine, and mine know me . . . and I lay down my life for my sheep. And other sheep I have that are not of this fold: them also I must bring, and they shall hear my voice, and there shall be one fold and one shepherd."[156]

[155]John 11:49-52.
[156]John 10:14-16.

The Mystery and Destiny of the Church

Since the Church is the household of God on earth, all nations are destined to be involved in its mystery. And if, for a time, God chose one people to be especially his own, it was only in order to achieve the salvation of all mankind by means of this Chosen People. Ultimately he would redeem all men, and his salvation would include the whole earth, not just the Chosen People.

During his public life, Jesus frequently spoke of the universal dimension of his salvation — as, for example, when he said to the Samaritan woman: "Woman, believe me, the hour is coming and now is, when you shall neither on this mountain, nor in Jerusalem, adore the Father, but the true adorers shall adore the Father in spirit and in truth. For the Father seeks such to adore him. God is a spirit: and they that adore him must adore him in spirit and in truth."[157] Nevertheless he reminded her that salvation was to come through the Chosen People,[158] and later the Apostles would be commissioned by Jesus to preach his gospel to the whole world, beginning at Jerusalem.[159]

Again, when explaining the mystery of the Church, Jesus always used parables that would convey the idea of universality, such as the net cast into the sea gathering all kinds of fishes, or the tiny mustard seed that grew into a great tree, or the yeast that permeated the flour. This was to be the nature of the Church, something like the mystery of the wheat field that is planted in the spring and grows slowly toward its perfection in the harvest time. Indeed, Jesus actually made the comparison himself when speaking of the nature of the Church to his disciples. He said: "So is the kingdom of God, as if a man should cast seed into the earth and

[157]John 4:21, 23-24.
[158]John 4:22.
[159]Luke 24:47.

should sleep and rise night and day, and the seed should spring and grow up while he knows it not. For the earth of itself brings forth fruit, first the blade, then the ear, afterward the full corn in the ear. And when the fruit is brought forth, immediately he puts in the sickle because the harvest has come."[160]

From the dawn of human history, God had been preparing the world for its ultimate unification in the mystery of the Church, and now he sent his Son to complete his work, as Jesus himself said: "My meat is to do the will of him who sent me, that I may perfect his work."[161]

When describing the nature of the Church, the symbol he employed most frequently was that of a kingdom. He spoke of it as the kingdom of God upon earth, the new spiritual Israel of which he himself was to be the king. The mystery of the kingdom of the Church was shown to the apostle John in his vision on Patmos, describing which he said: "I saw the heavens opened, and behold, a white horse, and he that sat upon him was called 'faithful and true'; and with justice does he judge and fight. And his eyes were as a flame of fire, and on his head were many diadems. And he had a name written, which no man knows but himself; and he was clothed with a garment sprinkled with blood; and his name is called: the Word of God."[162]

Of this kingdom Jesus himself was to be the architect;[163] but to assist him in the work of building and governing he chose twelve men whom he called Apostles to carry on the work of his Church and to spread his gospel to the ends of the earth when he should

[160]Mark 4:26-29.
[161]John 4:34.
[162]Apoc. 19:11-13 (RSV = Rev. 19:11-13).
[163]Cf. Heb. 3:1-6.

have returned to the Father after having accomplished the work of redemption.

It was still early in the public life, about June of the year AD 28, according to the general opinion of exegetes, when he set his hand to this all-important task. Recounting the event, the Evangelists say that one morning at dawn, Jesus stood on a mountainside surrounded by a throng of his disciples, after having spent the night in prayer to God, "and he chose from among them twelve men whom he named apostles."[164] "And he made that these should be with him and that he might send them to preach. And he gave them power to heal the sick and to cast out devils."[165] St. Matthew's description of this divine investiture of the Twelve with the powers of their apostolic office is particularly impressive. He said: "Heal the sick, raise the dead, cleanse the lepers, cast out devils. Freely have you received, freely give."[166]

With the choosing of the Apostles, Jesus had formally laid the foundation of his Church. The names of the Twelve Apostles thus chosen were Peter and Andrew, brothers; James and John, brothers; Philip and Bartholomew, friends; Thomas and Matthew; James the Less and his brother Jude (Thaddeus); Simon the Zealot, and Judas the traitor.[167]

Why Jesus chose these twelve from among all his other followers will forever remain the secret of his own divine counsel. The number twelve was symbolic in Scripture and signified the perfecting of a mysterious work of God. His choice of them was not based on any human consideration, such as personal excellence or

---

[164]Cf. Luke 6:12-13.
[165]Cf. Mark 3:14-15.
[166]Matt. 10:8.
[167]Cf. Matt. 10:2-4.

merit, for time was to reveal that, collectively speaking, they were a typical cross-section of human society, possessing an ample share of human shortcomings, yet fundamentally men of goodwill. St. Mark hints at the mystery of the divine choice when he says that "Jesus called unto him whom he would himself; and they came to him."[168]

Nowhere in the Gospels, perhaps, is the mystery of a divine vocation so clearly seen as in this selection of the Twelve. On the one hand, we see the sovereign freedom of Jesus inviting these men to follow him, his choice governed by reasons known to him alone; on the other hand, there was the free and willing response of the Twelve to the destiny held out to them. It was no human consideration that led them to accept the divine invitation at that hour, but rather, the divine fascination of the Godhead that was drawing them to Jesus; and it was his enlightening and sustaining grace that enabled them at that decisive moment to give a full and perfect assent to the divine call. By his grace they were convinced of the truth of his claims and were totally committed to his cause. Ultimately all but one of them would lay down their lives in testimony of their faith in him. Judas Iscariot alone would prove faithless to the point of betraying him to death. His place would be filled by Matthias, in order that the mystic number twelve would be preserved intact.[169]

As Jesus stood on the hillside in the radiant light of dawn on that eventful morning, surrounded by his chosen phalanx of Apostles, the silent multitude from whose ranks they had just been taken suddenly witnessed the ancient prophecy of Isaiah concerning the Church come to life: "Behold, I have graven you in my

[168]Mark 3:13.
[169]Cf. Acts 1:15-26.

hands, your walls are always before my eyes. Your builders are come! . . . Behold, I will lay your stones in order and will lay your foundations with sapphires. And I will make your bulwarks of jasper, and your gates of graven stones. All your children shall be taught by the Lord, and great shall be the peace of your children . . . No weapon that is formed against you shall prosper, and every tongue that resists you in judgment you shall condemn."[170]

These twelve predestined men who surrounded Jesus like a personal honor guard on the hillside that very morning were to be the twelve pillars upon which the Church of Christ would rest, just as the Church of the Old Covenant had rested on the twelve sons of Jacob. They were destined to become the twelve foundation stones of the New Jerusalem, the City of God, as it was shown to the apostle in his vision on Patmos.[171] Henceforth they would be known to all ages as the Twelve Apostles of Christ.

As they stood there, however, in the presence of the wondering multitude, they themselves did not grasp the true dimension of their vocation. It was only before his Ascension that Jesus would reveal it to them, when he would commission them to go forth and preach his gospel to every creature.[172] With that solemn mandate the Church would set forth on her final journey through time.

[170]Isa. 49:16-17; 54:11-13, 17.
[171]Apoc. 21:14 (RSV = Rev. 21:14).
[172]Matt. 28:18-20; Mark 16:16; Luke 24:46-49; John 20:21; Acts 1:4-8.

Chapter 21

The Twelve Apostles of Christ

It is interesting now to contemplate in retrospect the destinies of these twelve men as history later revealed it. Peter, who would later be constituted by Jesus head of the apostolic college, is always named first in the list of the apostles. The Gospels reveal him as a man of very forthright opinion and precipitous action; with him, to think was to act, and he often acted more from impulse than from conviction. Yet he was a man of sterling character, capable of profound and enduring affection. He was the type of character who could prove capable of the most devoted loyalty to one whom he really loved, and who would spare no effort to give manifest proof thereof.

Side by side with these great natural virtues, however, there were inherent defects, such as characterize that particular type of temperament. Peter was undoubtedly conscious of his great capacity for love but totally unaware of his natural weakness when confronted with grave danger. Indeed we could say that he had no real idea of his moral weakness but had perhaps an exaggerated idea of his moral strength. Yet the later discovery of his weakness would ultimately teach him compassion for others; and it might have been that because of his very character, Jesus would make him the chief shepherd of his entire flock.

Andrew, the brother of Peter, seems to have been more reserved in character than Peter. From the fleeting glimpses of him that the Gospels afford, we know that he was one of those devout Israelites who were looking for the kingdom of God,[173] deeply devoted to the religion of Israel. He had the singular privilege of being one of the first two disciples to follow Jesus, yet he gets relatively little attention in the subsequent unfolding of the Gospel story. After the first Pentecost, he preached the gospel in Scythia, Thrace, and Greece, where he ultimately sealed the testimony of his faith by martyrdom.[174]

James the Greater, the brother of John, is so called to distinguish him from the other apostle James, who is commonly called "the Less." Despite the fact that he was one of the three most beloved disciples, there is only one brief sentence of his recorded in the Gospels. This isolated remark was made as Jesus was passing through Samaria on his way to Jerusalem, when the Samaritans refused to receive Jesus, precisely because he was on his way to the Holy City. Indignant at such discourteous behavior, James and his brother John asked Jesus if they could use their apostolic powers to destroy the offenders by calling down fire and brimstone to consume them.[175] This reaction showed their typically Galilean temperament and caused Jesus to name them "sons of thunder."[176]

He seems to have shared the prevalent although erroneous concept of the Messiah as a conquering king who would free the people from the tyranny of foreign aggression, for he was ambitious enough to consent to his mother's formal request to Jesus

---

[173]Cf. Luke 23:51.

[174]*Breviary of the Order of Preachers*, Pt. I (Dublin: St. Savior's, 1967), 794 ff.

[175]Luke 9:54.

[176]Mark 3:17.

that he and his brother John be nominated to the highest places in the kingdom.[177]

After Pentecost, Andrew evangelized Spain and, upon his return to Jerusalem, was slain by the sword in AD 42 by order of King Agrippa I, grandson of Herod the Great and brother of Herodias, the woman who contrived the death of John the Baptist, through her daughter Salome. It was on that occasion that Agrippa had Peter imprisoned also, intending to have him likewise executed after the Passover, but the overruling Providence of God intervened to save him for a more glorious combat later on, so he was released from prison by an angel.[178] James was the first of the Twelve to be martyred, and he suffered death in Jerusalem, like his namesake and fellow apostle, James the Less, in the year 62.

John, the brother of James the Greater, was one of the first two disciples to follow Jesus.[179] He is believed to have been the youngest of the Twelve, and perhaps the only unmarried member of the apostolic group. He was especially loved by Jesus because of his singular purity of heart. The Gospels reveal him as being of a reserved disposition, although, as the incident with the Samaritans shows, he was capable of quick and violent action on occasion. Endowed with a keen intellect, he also was gifted with the loftiness of vision and deep spiritual insight of a poet.

On Calvary he stood with Mary, the mother of Jesus, at the foot of the Cross, and received from Jesus the singular privilege of being her earthly guardian after his death. From the Cross Jesus likewise entrusted the whole human race, in the person of John, to his

[177]Matt. 20:20-23.
[178]Acts 12:1-10.
[179]John 1:35-40.

mother's care, and bade mankind, in the person of John, to accept her as mother.

About sixty or seventy years after the death of Jesus, John wrote his Gospel. And about the same time, he wrote the book of Revelation, or the Apocalypse, about AD 95. This book records the visions he received on the island of Patmos, to which he had been banished by order of the Roman emperor Domitian.[180] This book contains many mysterious revelations about the destiny of the Church in the last ages of the world.

John is the only one of the Twelve who did not die a martyr's death, although he is said to have suffered the torments of martyrdom during the persecution of the Christians by the Roman empire. He is believed to have died during the reign of the emperor Trajan, about the year 100 and to have been buried near the city of Ephesus.

Philip the apostle was a native of Bethsaida, a town on the north shore of the Sea of Galilee. He figures in the Gospel scene, although he was not a prominent member of the apostolic college. Of a mild and peaceful disposition, he was always easy of approach, ready to render a helpful service in case of need. He is believed to have preached the gospel in the region of the Black Sea, in Scythia and Asia Minor, and to have met his death by crucifixion.[181]

Bartholomew, or Nathanael, was a native of Cana of Galilee, a village about four miles to the northeast of Nazareth. His call by Jesus is related in detail by John, but after this he remains in obscurity throughout the public life of Jesus. He is mentioned again in the forty-day period after the Resurrection, being one of the seven

[180]*Breviary of the Order of Preachers*, Pt. I, 839.
[181]Ibid., 1065.

disciples to whom Jesus showed himself by the lakeshore one morning at dawn after they had spent a night in fruitless toil fishing. He was, therefore, one of the witnesses of the solemn investiture of Peter, by Jesus, as Head of the Church on earth.[182]

On the testimony of Jesus himself we know that Bartholomew was a man of guileless heart, a sincere and devout Israelite, although the Gospels also reveal that he was a typical Galilean with very strong prejudices and very definite opinions, yet completely loyal once he had been won over to a cause. He is believed to have preached the gospel in the region of Armenia, where he was ultimately martyred for the faith, by being flayed alive.[183]

Thomas the apostle is one of the less well known of the Twelve. How or when he first met Jesus is not recorded in the Gospels, but he is believed to have been a Galilean, as all the others were, with the exception of Judas. The Gospels reveal him as being rather stubborn, one who could not be easily prevailed upon to alter his convictions, yet beneath the surface of his rock-like nature, he had an affectionate heart and a deeply sincere soul. He was the type of person who could pledge himself with utter dedication to an ideal once he had been convinced of its worth. He scorned danger, as we see at the close of Jesus' public life when he proposed to return to Jerusalem and the disciples were afraid to follow; they knew that death and danger would attend every step of the way thither, but Thomas rose to the occasion and said: "Let us also go, that we may die with him."[184]

True to his nature, he stubbornly refused to believe in the Resurrection of Jesus, except on his own terms. "Except I shall see in

[182]John 21.
[183]*Breviary of the Order of Preachers*, Pt. II, 721.
[184]John 11:16.

his hands the print of the nails, and put my finger into the place of the nails and put my hand into his side, I will not believe." A week later, Jesus took him at his word and invited him to come forward and fulfill his own requirements. He said to him: " 'Put in your finger here and see my hands. And bring hither your hand and put it into my side. And be not faithless, but believing.' Thomas answered and said to him: 'My Lord and my God!' "[185] Evidently he accepted the challenge and was completely won over by what he found; instantly he hastened to make amends for his former disbelief by this marvelous profession of faith, which wonderfully sums up the character of the one who made it. Thomas preached the gospel in Parthia and India and was martyred there for the faith by being pierced through with javelins.[186]

Matthew the publican is called Levi by Mark and by Luke, probably out of consideration for this once-despised member of Israel's society.[187] After the beautiful account of his call by Jesus, the Gospels lapse into silence and there is not a single word of his recorded by the Evangelists. But although he remained in the shadows, so to speak, he was not idle. His former profession as tax collector gave him a businesslike sense of order and method, and unknown to anyone, he put these talents to good use, in a very different field. He noted carefully the words and actions of Jesus, gathered every available scrap of authentic information about his words and works previous to his own call, and even collected reliable and detailed information concerning Jesus' origin, birth, and infancy, all of which he ultimately gave to the Church in that testament of immortal beauty which we call St. Matthew's Gospel.

[185]John 20:25, 27-28.
[186]*Breviary of the Order of Preachers*, Pt. I, 824.
[187]Mark 2:14; Luke 5:27.

Many exegetes believe that Matthew was the first of the four Evangelists to write the Gospel; if he was not the first, he certainly was the second. He first wrote it in Aramaic sometime between the years 50 and 55, which was about twenty or twenty-five years after the Crucifixion. Less than twenty years later, it was translated into Greek. The words of unfading beauty in which he has recorded the life and teachings of Christ have enshrined the name and memory of the once-despised publican in the light of immortal glory. After the first Pentecost, Matthew preached the gospel in Ethiopia, where he ultimately suffered martyrdom while celebrating the Eucharist.[188]

James the Less, the brother of John, was a kinsman of Jesus. He is one of the less well known members of the apostolic college, for nothing of his words or deeds is recorded in the Gospels. After the Ascension of Jesus, he was appointed Bishop of Jerusalem, an office he held for over thirty years. A person of great austerity of life, he was revered by Jews and Christians alike for his spirit of prayer and penance. In the year 62, about thirty-two years after the Crucifixion, he suffered martyrdom for his constant preaching of Christ as the Son of God. He was first stoned and then cast headlong from the pinnacle of the temple, then finally killed by a blow on the head from a fuller's club.[189]

Jude, surnamed Thaddeus, meaning "stout," was a brother of James the Less, and therefore a near relative of Jesus.[190] Little is known about him except his call to the apostleship. He was one of those who addressed Jesus during the discourse at the Last Supper, and he is the author of the letter that bears his name. He preached

---

[188]*Breviary of the Order of Preachers*, Pt. II, 789.

[189]Ibid., Pt. I, 1066.

[190]Cf. Luke 6:16.

the gospel in Mesopotamia and Persia, where he was ultimately crowned with martyrdom together with the apostle Simon.[191]

Simon called "the Cananean" by Sts. Matthew and Mark, is called *Zealotes*[192] by St. Luke. He is the least known of all the apostles, since not a single word or action of his is recorded in the Gospels. After Pentecost he preached the gospel in Egypt, but later went to Persia, where he was united with Jude in the evangelization of that nation. Ultimately they were both crowned with martyrdom in that region.[193]

Last on the list of the apostles is Judas Iscariot, who betrayed Jesus. He is believed to have been the only one of the Twelve who was not a native of Galilee. His surname designates the place of his family origin, which is likely to have been the village of Carioth in the tribal territory of Judah. It is mentioned in the book of Joshua,[194] but it has not yet been identified. It is quite possible, however, that Judas himself had been living in Galilee like the other apostles for some time prior to his call by Jesus. It is not known how or where he first met Jesus, or what motives prompted him initially to cast his lot with him. Whatever his motives, even if they were not of the most disinterested kind, he must have been sincere in his desire to follow him in the beginning. The Gospels reveal that he gradually drifted away from Jesus in spirit, even though he continued outwardly as a member of the apostolic

---

[191]*Breviary of the Order of Preachers*, Pt. II, 789.

[192]Ibid., 879. Many scholars think it is unlikely that the apostle Simon belonged to the fanatical political group known as Zealots: the name zealot probably indicated a personal trait of character, or his zeal for the Law (cf. *Catholic Commentary*, sect. 728i).

[193]*Breviary of the Order of Preachers*, Pt. II, 879.

[194]Josh. 15:25.

group, until he finally abandoned him and handed him over to his enemies. This final tragedy led him to despair and death on the very day that Jesus himself died for the salvation of the world.

These manifold destinies were hidden, however, within the impenetrable veil of the future on that sunlit morning when Jesus stood on the mountainside crowned with the aureola of his Apostles. It will be of interest now to look more deeply into the mystery of their mission and vocation in the Church.

Chapter 22

The Teaching and Governing Church

Since God ordained that all men should be brought to share the fruits of redemption through the Church established by his beloved Son, Jesus constituted the Church as a visible society that it might be manifest to all. Such visibility was necessary so that any honest inquirer might be led to find the truth in all its fullness in the Church of Christ alone. What Jesus said of the individual disciple is preeminently true of the Church as a visible society or institution: "A city seated on a mountain cannot be hid. Neither do men light a candle and put it under a bushel, but upon a candlestick, that it may shine to all that are in the house."[195] The Church of Christ is truly that city.

In order to ensure that his Church would endure through all ages, unchanged by the ravages of time and impregnable against the assaults of its enemies, Jesus consolidated its strength by a well-ordered system of government and endowed it with other gifts of grace by which men of all ages would be enabled to recognize it as "his Church." To this end he established a definite hierarchy or order of authority within the apostolic college which he had chosen to assist him in its foundation and government. Thus, he invested Peter with the office of supreme authority in the

---

[195]Matt. 5:14-15.

Church, appointing him Chief Shepherd of his entire flock, both the hierarchy and the simple faithful.[196]

The first intimation of Peter's singular destiny was given by Jesus at his first meeting with his apostle, who was at that time called Simon. Jesus, looking upon him, said: "You are Simon the Son of Jona. You shall be called Cephas, which is interpreted Peter."[197] Then, as the public life began to unfold, he continued to give Peter priority of place among the Twelve, as though to focus attention on his future destiny in the mystery of the Church. Thus, for example, in the mysterious episode of the miraculous draught of fishes, he singled out Peter for leadership, for it was to him that Jesus said: "Launch out into the deep and let down your nets for a draught."[198] And it was Peter's net that enclosed the miraculous catch; it was to Peter, moreover, that Jesus said: "From henceforth you shall catch men."[199] Throughout his public life, Jesus addressed the multitudes on the shore from Peter's boat or plied the waters of the lake on the various journeys of his gospel ministry.

The great revelation of Peter's future vocation was not given until the public life was at its height, perhaps about July of the year AD 29, in the neighborhood of Caesarea Philippi, in the northeastern section of the nation that was the territory of Philip the tetrarch. There Jesus asked his Apostles who the public, at large, thought he was. " 'Who do men say that the Son of Man is?' They replied: 'Some John the Baptist, and others Elias, and others Jeremiah or one of the prophets.' 'But who do you say that I am?' he

---

[196]Cf. Matt. 16:13-19; John 21:15-17.
[197]John 1:42.
[198]Luke 5:4.
[199]Cf. Luke 5:10.

continued. Simon Peter answered and said: 'You are Christ, the Son of the living God.' "[200]

Jesus was deeply gratified by the apostle's forthright confession and rewarded it with a divine munificence. He replied: "Blessed are you, Simon Bar-Jona: because flesh and blood has not revealed it to you, but my Father who is in heaven. And I say to you: That you are Peter, and upon this rock I will build my church. And the gates of hell shall not prevail against it. And I will give to you the keys of the kingdom of heaven. And whatsoever you shall bind upon earth it shall be bound also in heaven; and whatsoever you shall loose on earth, it shall be loosed also in heaven."[201]

This formal promise signified that Peter was destined to be invested with the office of supreme authority in the Church on earth. For as yet it was only a promise. In every civilized society, the keys symbolize the office of supreme authority. True to his word, Jesus fulfilled this promise after his Resurrection, for one morning at dawn, by the shore of the lake there occurred an incident that John recounts in his Gospel.

It was sometime during the forty-day period between the Resurrection and the Ascension. Seven of the apostles were returning toward the shore after having spent a fruitless night fishing on the lake. As they came nearer the land, they saw a man standing on the shore, but they did not recognize him. When he learned of their disappointment, he told them to cast the net on the right side of the ship and they would make a catch. They did so, and at once enclosed such a great number of fish that they could scarcely bring the net to shore. It was only then that they recognized the stranger as Jesus.

[200]Matt. 16:13-16.
[201]Matt. 16:17-19.

The Mystery and Destiny of the Church

Immediately Peter cast himself into the sea to come to him, while the other disciples followed after in the boat, dragging the net. When they reached the shore, Jesus asked them to bring some of the fish they had caught; there were 153. In this mysterious incident, symbolic of the future apostolic activity of the Church, it was Peter who took the initiative to bring the fish to Jesus, and it was then that Jesus invited them to partake of the breakfast he had prepared for them.

When they had finished, he entered into a mysterious dialogue with Peter while the others looked on in solemn silence. "Simon, son of John, do you love me more then these?" he asked. To which Peter replied with confidence: "Yes, Lord, you know that I love you." Jesus replied in turn: "Feed my lambs." A second time he repeated the question, and a second time Peter gave the selfsame reply. Yet a third time Jesus questioned him: "Simon, son of John, do you love me?" Peter was grieved by this third repetition of the question, and he replied as though doubting his own heart: "Lord, you know all things; you know that I love you." And Jesus said to him: "Feed my sheep."[202]

Thus, in the presence of the other six apostles, Jesus solemnly invested Peter with the office of Supreme Pastor of his Church, entrusting to him the care of his entire flock, both pastors and simple faithful. Some are inclined to see in the lambs a symbol of the simple faithful, and in the sheep, a symbol of the hierarchy or official governors of the Church. Since the Law declared that in the mouth of two or three witnesses every word shall stand,[203] this solemn investiture of Peter as Supreme Pastor of the flock of Christ marked the formal establishment of the hierarchy of the Church.

[202]Cf. John 21:15-17.
[203]Deut. 17:6.

According to the disposition of Jesus, Peter was appointed leader of the apostolic college. While the other apostles shared the apostolic powers and were destined to become co-builders of the Church with him, they were nevertheless to work subject to his authority and direction, and never independently of him. Thus, the Twelve, under the direction of Peter, were to govern the Church until the end of time, for through their lawful successors, this hierarchy of authority as designed by Christ was to continue unchanged until his Second Coming. It has been preserved intact to this day in the Roman Catholic Church.

It was necessary that such a hierarchy of authority should exist within the Church, since even in secular society, the supreme governing power in any institution must ultimately reside in one person, if the institution as such is to survive. Any violation of this principle inevitably leads to anarchy, division, and ultimate disintegration. This hierarchical structure of the Church as designed by Jesus, and the prerogative of place and office that it conferred on Peter were recognized and accepted without question in the early Church.

The authority vested in this power, passed also to the other apostles, and the institution established by this decree, has been continued in all the leaders of the Church. But it is not without good reason that what is bestowed on all is entrusted to one. For Peter received it separately in trust, because he is the prototype set before all the rulers of the Church.

Having completed the work of founding the Church, he gave his Apostles a formal mandate to preach his gospel to the whole world. This event occurred sometime during the forty-day period between the Resurrection and the Ascension and is described by Matthew in the last chapter of his Gospel. Describing the scene, the apostle says: "The eleven disciples went into Galilee, unto the mountain where Jesus had appointed them. And Jesus, coming, spoke to them, saying: All power is given to me in heaven and on earth. Going, therefore, teach all nations, baptizing them in the name of the Father and of the Son and of the Holy Spirit, teaching them to observe all things whatsoever I have commanded you. And behold, I am with you all days, even to the consummation of the world."[204] With this formal mandate, Jesus invested his Apostles with the official teaching and governing offices of his Church and made them the official guardians and interpreters of divine revelation in every age to come. This official teaching office of the Church is called the Magisterium.

---

[204]Matt. 28:16-20.

Chapter 23

The Magisterium of the Church

The extraordinary nature of this office required an extraordinary fullness of grace on the part of Peter, the Supreme Pontiff, and the other members of the apostolic college. For if they were constituted the official custodians, interpreters, and teachers of divine revelation, charged with bringing the fullness of truth to men, it was absolutely necessary that they be preserved from error in their teaching. Jesus himself guaranteed this fullness of grace, first by his solemn promise to remain always with his Church,[205] and secondly by his promise to send the Holy Spirit to guide and enlighten them in the discharge of this sacred office.

He said:

> I will not leave you orphans. I will ask the Father, and he shall give you another Paraclete, that he may abide with you forever, the Spirit of truth whom the world cannot receive, because it does not see him or know him, but you shall know him; because he shall abide with you and shall be in you . . . But the Paraclete, the Holy Spirit, whom the Father will send in my name, he will teach you all things, and bring all things to your mind, whatsoever I shall have said to you . . . But when he, the Spirit of truth is come, he

[205]Matt. 28:20.

will teach you all truth. For he shall not speak of himself; but what things soever he shall hear, he shall speak, and the things that are to come, he shall show you . . . But when the Paraclete comes, whom I will send you from the Father, the Spirit of truth, who proceeds from the Father, he shall give testimony of me: And you shall give testimony, because you are with me from the beginning.[206]

Upon this twofold promise of Christ — namely, the promise of his own abiding presence within the Church and the guiding and enlightening presence of the Holy Spirit — rests the Church's teaching of the doctrine and dogma of infallibility.

For the Church holds that by reason of these, and other such extraordinary promises, and the graces they infer, Jesus has made her infallible — that is, incapable of teaching error or falsehood. Infallibility follows naturally from the very nature of the teaching office committed to Peter and the apostles, as inevitably as the effect springs from its cause.

The Church exercises her infallible authority in three ways:

• In the voice of the Pope, the Bishop of Rome, the Vicar of Christ, and Supreme Shepherd or Pastor of the universal Church, when he speaks *ex cathedra* — that is, when he actually exercises his office as divinely authorized teacher of the Church.

• In the voice of the bishops when they are assembled in a General (Ecumenical) Council, with the Pope at their head.

• In the voice of the bishops dispersed throughout the world with the Pope at their head.

[206]John 14:18, 26; 16:13; 15:26-27.

The Magisterium of the Church

The Supreme Pontiff — that is, the Pope — is infallible when he speaks *ex cathedra*, meaning from St. Peter's Chair. We say that he speaks *ex cathedra* 1) when he speaks as head of the Church, not as a private priest or bishop; 2) when he defines a doctrine, not merely expresses an opinion or preaches a sermon; 3) when he teaches on faith and morals, not about science or human knowledge; and 4) when he declares a doctrine as binding on all the faithful — that is, a doctrine, not as useful or desirable but as a truth that all must believe.

We see from this that the doctrine of infallibility as held and interpreted by the Church is eminently reasonable. It is absolutely necessary for the preservation of true doctrine that such a grace should be given to the Supreme Pastor of the Church, for without it, the truth and integrity of the faith would be quickly obscured and ultimately lost.

The official teaching office of the Church belongs exclusively to the Supreme Pontiff and to the bishops in communion with him. While theologians or scholars in other fields may render useful and valuable service in the elucidation of Sacred Scripture, their role, however praiseworthy, is by the very nature of the case, a secondary one. For the deposit of divine revelation contains many elements of mystery which are altogether beyond the scope or competence of human scholarship to determine. These dark regions of mystery, so to speak, lie beyond the frontiers of human speculation, beyond the range of the dynamo of human reason. Only the light of divine revelation can illumine these dark regions of mystery; and this light resides in the teaching Magisterium of the Church alone.

Chapter 24

The Seven Sacraments of the Church

Among the most important means that Jesus has given his Church to enable Man to receive copiously of the graces of redemption, the seven sacraments are worthy of special mention. They might be compared to seven fountains of living waters in the kingdom of God,[207] or seven streams that flow from the mystic river of Eden, to irrigate the face of the redeemed earth with the waters of grace.[208] For the seven sacraments provide for every spiritual necessity of Man, just as food, drink, medicine, clothing, and shelter provide for his material needs. The seven sacraments are Baptism, Confirmation, Eucharist, Penance (Reconciliation), Anointing (the Sacrament of the Sick), Holy Orders, and Matrimony.

The Church defines a sacrament as an outward sign instituted by Christ to give grace to the soul.[209] Three things are necessary to make a sacrament: an outward sign, grace, and institution by Christ. The word *sacrament* signifies a means to holiness. Let us now briefly consider the three requisites for a sacrament.

First, there must be an outward sign. A sign is that by which a thing is made known. For example, smoke indicates fire; the

[207]Cf. Isa. 12:3.

[208]Cf. Gen. 2:6-10.

[209]For a basic study of the sacraments in general, see *Baltimore Catechism*, no. 3, 69 ff.; for an in-depth study, see *CCC*, 311 ff.; *Summa Theologica*, II, Q. 60 ff.

pouring of the water on the head of a person in Baptism indicates the cleansing of the soul from sin. If a sign also produces the thing it makes known, it is an effective sign — that is, a sacrament.

A sacrament is a sacred action combined with appropriate words. By means of a sacrament, grace is made known, and grace is also given. The ceremonies surrounding the sacred action were added by the Church. These ceremonies have a twofold purpose: to enkindle devotion and to explain the sacraments. Jesus instituted seven sacraments; each sacrament is mentioned in the Bible, although the Bible does not say when exactly some of the sacraments were instituted. Baptism gives supernatural life to the soul; Confirmation strengthens that life; the Holy Eucharist nourishes it; Reconciliation restores it; Anointing protects it to the end; Holy Orders provides ministers for the sacraments and for the service of the church, to teach, to rule, and to instruct; Matrimony (Marriage) sanctifies married life. Thus, the sacraments minister to all our spiritual needs.

Let us now look more closely at each sacrament. As we have said, every sacrament must have three basic requisites: it must be an outward sign, it must confer grace, and it must have been instituted by Christ and no one else. The outward sign consists of the matter and form of the sacrament. The matter is the thing used and the actions performed in conferring the sacrament. The form is the words said.

The grace conferred by the sacrament is the effect of the sacrament, or what happens in the soul when the outward sign is correctly administered.

The "Divine Institution" of the sacrament means that it must have been instituted by Christ to give grace to the soul. Jesus instituted the Seven sacraments during his public life and during the forty days after his Resurrection.

The sacraments have power to give grace, from the merits of Christ; they are divided into two classes: sacraments of the living and sacraments of the dead. The sacraments of the living are so called because the soul must be alive, or in the state of grace, in order to receive them worthily. These five sacraments are Confirmation, Eucharist, Anointing (of the sick), Holy Orders, and Matrimony.

The sacraments of the dead are so called because they raise the soul from the death of sin to the life of grace; that is actually their function. These two sacraments are Baptism and Penance (or Reconciliation). The minister of the sacraments is the person who gives or administers them. The ordinary minister is the person who gives a sacrament, the one who gives it in his own right. An extraordinary minister is one who gives a sacrament by special permission, an unusual minister.

When there is question of receiving a sacrament, we say that a sacrament should be received in two ways: validly and lawfully. A sacrament is validly — that is, really — received when the matter and form are rightly given by the proper minister to a person who is capable and willing to receive it. A sacrament is lawfully — that is, fruitfully — received when a person is in the proper dispositions to get the grace of the sacrament. By the proper dispositions we mean the condition one's soul is in, or the way in which one prepares to receive the sacraments. A sacrament can be validly administered and yet no grace be given if the person receiving the sacrament did not have the proper dispositions; this would be the fault of the receiver. In such a case, the sacrament would be received unlawfully.

The sacraments work in the soul by their own power. Our dispositions do not produce the grace; they only allow the sacrament to act, or prevent it from acting, as the case may be.

We may have perfect dispositions if we do all we can to prepare well for a sacrament, and in this case, we shall receive a great abundance of grace. We may have, on the contrary, sufficient dispositions if we do only what is necessary to receive the sacrament worthily; in this case, we still receive grace but not the great abundance that perfect dispositions would merit. Finally, we may have bad dispositions if we receive a sacrament unworthily — that is, in a state of mortal sin, or without doing what is absolutely necessary to prepare ourselves for a lawful reception of the sacrament. In such a case, we would receive no grace at all; rather, we would be guilty of a sacrilege.

As regards the minister of the sacrament, his worthiness or unworthiness does not affect the sacrament. All that is required of him, in this context, is that he perform the sacramental action as prescribed by the Church and have the intention of doing what the Church intends. If he does this, the sacrament is validly administered, and its fruitfulness depends upon our own dispositions.

We have mentioned that some of the sacraments give or restore sanctifying grace to the soul when grace has been lost or is absent; this is their specific function. These sacraments are Baptism and Penance. When their reception is not possible, in the case of Baptism, the sacrament can be replaced by "Baptism of Desire" — that is, the explicit or implicit wish for Baptism, with perfect contrition for sin — or, in the case of Penance, the sacrament can be replaced by an act of perfect contrition for sin. In these two sacraments of Baptism and Penance, Jesus raises the spiritually dead to life, as he raised the physically dead to life while on earth.

The other five sacraments — Confirmation, Eucharist, Anointing, Holy Orders, and Matrimony — increase the sanctifying grace already in the soul. The names of these five sacraments show that they were instituted for a special purpose, and not for the taking away of sin.

Besides giving sanctifying grace to the soul, the sacraments also give another grace, which is called sacramental grace. This grace is a special help that is given by God to attain the end for which he instituted each sacrament. If the sacraments gave only sanctifying grace, one sacrament alone would have been sufficient.

The sacraments always give grace if we receive them with the right dispositions. The right disposition for the valid reception of any sacrament is an intention to receive that sacrament. In addition, we must receive Baptism before we may receive any other sacrament. The Baptism and Holy Communion of infants exclude the necessity of intention.

The right dispositions for a lawful — that is, fruitful or licit — reception of the sacraments are, in the case of Baptism and Penance, a pure intention and an act of Contrition. In the case of the other sacraments, a pure intention and freedom form mortal sin, which means to be in the state of grace.

Of the seven sacraments, three — namely, Baptism, Confirmation, and Holy Orders — can be received only once, because they imprint upon the soul a special mark or character that can never be effaced. Since this mark or character can never be destroyed, the sacrament that gives it need not and may not be received a second time.

The character is not a grace but a spiritual distinction given to the soul. Thus, Baptism gives the character of a child of God — that is, it distinguishes us as children of God. Confirmation gives the character of a soldier of Christ, and Holy Orders gives the character of a priest of God. This remains in the soul even after death, for the honor and glory of those who are saved, but for the shame and punishment of those who are lost.

If Baptism, Confirmation, or Holy Orders are received unworthily, the grace of the sacrament is suspended, or held over, until the sin is removed. The same may be said of the sacrament of Matrimony.

We cannot overestimate the importance of the sacraments, for they are at the very heart of the Church as one of the primary sources by which the faithful are sanctified and strengthened in their faith. Who would not be impressed by the liturgical ceremonies that accompany a solemn Baptism or the sacrament of Confirmation? Or who would not be moved by the splendor of ceremonial and song with which the Liturgy of the Eucharist is celebrated?

The Sacrifice of the Holy Eucharist is the center of the Church's liturgical worship, and more than all else, perhaps, proclaims the glory and majesty of the Catholic Faith.

The sacrament of Confession, or Reconciliation, is surrounded by the formal privacy that is required by its very nature, and here more than anywhere else, perhaps, we experience the power of binding and loosing that Christ granted to the Apostles.

The sacrament of Anointing helps individual souls to experience the love and mercy of God in their last hours. It calms the natural fear and anxiety that accompany the passage of the soul from time to eternity.

Holy Orders selects and trains the ministers of the Church, from the highest to the lowest ranks, and it is through this sacrament that the powers of the priesthood of the New Testament are transferred, or handed on, by the lawful authority of the Supreme Pontiff, the Vicar of Christ, to the various orders of the Church's governing and teaching body.

The seventh sacrament — Matrimony — is surrounded by the constant vigilance of the Church, in order to ensure that the union of husband and wife is blessed and that the dignity of human life in its every aspect is preserved and respected.

It is the ceremonial employed in the administration of the sacraments that has gradually developed the beautiful way of life that we call the Christian civilization which has become the precious patrimony of the Christian Church. And it is the administration of the sacraments that makes it possible to minister to every need of the faithful, whether of body or soul. It is, moreover, through the administration of the sacraments that the great precept of the New Law of Christ is daily brought to fulfillment: "A new commandment I give to you, that you love one another as I have loved you. By this shall all men know that you are my disciples: that you love one another."[210]

In view of what we have said of the sacraments in general, it will be helpful to consider very briefly some basic facts about the Holy Eucharist, leaving it to the reader to pursue the study of the other sacraments.

[210]John 13:34-35.

Chapter 25

The Eucharist

So much could be written about the sacrament of the Eucharist that it would fill a volume in itself. The most we can attempt here is to reflect briefly upon the most important theological teachings of the Church concerning it. But before beginning to speak of the nature and effects of this sacrament, we must first remember that when considering any aspect thereof, we are moving in the realm of mystery; and as in the case of all mystery, we reach a point at which all discussion becomes futile and all investigation inadequate. Because it is finite of its very nature, the mind reaches a frontier beyond which it cannot pass. In this sacrament we are dealing with the omnipotent power of God, with his creative power, and with the sovereign freedom of his divine will. He can act as he pleases, transcending his own laws for his own divine glory.

This most awesome sacrament contains not one, but many mysteries, which transcend the power of human reason to comprehend beyond a certain point. In trying to fathom it, we are in the same position as St. Augustine when he tried to fathom the mystery of the Blessed Trinity. As he walked along the seashore, absorbed in thought, he saw a child playing in the sand and asked him what he was doing. The child replied that he was trying to fit the ocean into a small hollow he had scooped out in the sand. "Oh," replied the saint, "you should know that this is impossible!"

"Then," replied the child, "you must also know that it is equally impossible to fathom the mystery of the Trinity," and so saying, he vanished.

Likewise, when trying to fathom the mystery of the Eucharist, we are confronted with the mystery of God himself, which is utterly beyond the powers of a finite intellect. For herein we have a mysterious presence of God, yet a very real presence, beneath what appears outwardly to be simply bread and wine; and it is the nature of this Real Presence of Jesus in this Blessed Sacrament that the Church sets herself to define, guided by the grace of the Holy Spirit in virtue of her teaching office.

In this matter, we must be very careful to abide by her official teaching, and the interpretation of this mystery, as set forth by her, is one instance in which the word of Jesus is literally fulfilled in his Church: "It is not you who speak but the Spirit of your Father that speaks in you."[211] It is likewise an instance in which Man must receive the word of God as a child.[212] What is supremely important to remember here is that when treating of this august sacrament, everything is pure fact. There is nothing symbolic, figurative, or any such thing in question; everything is real, although all is mystery.

Before beginning our reflections on the sacrament of the Eucharist itself, it may be well to speak for a moment about the person and nature of Jesus, for in this sacrament we are dealing directly with him. In the first chapter of his Gospel, St. John declared Jesus to be God, when he said: "In the beginning was the Word; and the Word was with God; and the Word was God. The same was in the beginning with God. All things were made by

---

[211]Matt. 10:20.
[212]Cf. Mark 10:15.

him: and without him was made nothing that was made . . . And the Word was made flesh and dwelt among us, and we saw his glory, the glory as it were of the only begotten of the Father, full of grace and truth."[213]

The Church formally took up this declaration of the inspired apostle and Evangelist, and officially proclaimed her faith in the divinity of Christ in the solemn and majestic opening phrases of the Nicene Creed:

> We believe in one God, the Father, the Almighty, maker of heaven and earth, of all that is seen and unseen. We believe in one Lord, Jesus Christ, the only Son of God, eternally begotten of the Father, God from God, Light from Light, true God from true God, begotten, not made, one in being with the Father. Through him all things were made. For us men and for our salvation he came down from heaven: by the power of the Holy Spirit he was born of the Virgin Mary, and became man.

We see from this that Jesus was no ordinary person, but awesome and profound in his being and nature. He was the Son of the eternal Father, made Man, true God and true Man.

The Gospel explicitly says that the reason for his coming was "to save his people from their sins."[214] This he did by his death on the Cross. But his death was not a permanent going away, for he willed to abide forever with his people, for whose salvation he offered himself as a victim to the eternal Father. This he did by means of the Eucharist, the sacrament of his abiding presence among men.

[213]John 1:1-3, 14.
[214]Matt. 1:21.

The Church defines the Holy Eucharist as the sacrament that contains the Body and Blood, Soul and Divinity of our Lord Jesus Christ under the appearances of bread and wine. Jesus instituted the sacrament of the Holy Eucharist at the Last Supper, on the night before he died. This was his last, or farewell, supper with his Apostles before his death. It was not an ordinary supper but the celebration of the Passover supper, and it brought the Old Testament or Covenant to a close.

Describing its institution, the Church tells us in the Gospels that on the night before his death, a Thursday, while he sat with his Apostles at the Last Supper, his enemies up the street were coordinating their final plans for his death; but he, at the same time, was devising a way by which he would remain with his people forever. The Gospels say that while they were at supper, Jesus took bread, blessed and broke it, and gave it to his disciples and said: "Take and eat; this is my body." And taking the chalice, he gave thanks and gave it to them, saying: "Drink ye all of this. For this is my blood of the new testament, which shall be shed for many for the remission of sins."[215]

St. Luke says that after he had consecrated the bread and wine, he added: "Do this for a commemoration of me."[216] It is the formal teaching of the Church that when Jesus pronounced these words over the bread and over the wine, he instituted the sacrament of the Holy Eucharist. When he said the words, "Do this for a commemoration of me," he ordained the Apostles as the first priests of the New Testament and established the Mass as the only Sacrifice in his Church. When he offered the consecrated bread and wine to the Apostles, which was now changed into his Body and

[215]Matt. 26:26-29; Mark 14:22-24.
[216]Luke 22:19.

Blood, he said Mass and distributed Holy Communion for the first time.

What happened when he said: "This is my Body; this is my Blood"? When he said over the bread: "This is my body," the substance of bread was changed into the substance of his Body; when he said over the wine: "This is my blood," the substance of the wine was changed into the substance of his Blood. Every created thing is composed of a substance and appearances. By *substance* we mean the thing itself, and by *appearances* we mean the qualities the thing has, to make it visible and known to us. Usually the substance and appearances are intimately united, but in the sacrament of the Eucharist, Jesus separates the two, and he himself takes the place of the substance of bread and wine. Now, Jesus Christ is whole and entire both under the form of bread and under the form of wine.

Where the Body of Christ is, there also is his Blood, because in the sacrament of the Holy Eucharist, we have the living Christ. After the substance of the bread and wine had been changed into the substance of the Body and Blood of Christ, there remained only the appearances of bread and wine. By the *appearances* of bread and wine we mean the shape, the color, the taste, and whatever appears to the senses of hearing, sight, smell, taste, and touch. This changing of the bread and wine into the Body and Blood of Christ is called *Transubstantiation*, which means changing from one substance into another. It is the wonderful and singular change of the whole substance of bread into the substance of the Body of Christ, and the whole substance of wine into the substance of his Blood, with only the appearances of bread and wine remaining.

In the course of the centuries, some heretics have taught that the Body of Christ and the substance of bread exist together. This is a false doctrine, called *consubstantiation*, which means substances existing with each other. It is condemned by the Church.

The Church formally teaches that Jesus Christ, true God and true Man, is really present with his Body and Blood, his Soul and Divinity, under the appearances of bread and wine. This is what is called the doctrine of the Real Presence. It is an article of Faith. Each species is a real sacrament — that is, the bread that has been consecrated into his Body, and the wine that has been consecrated into his Blood. And Christ is present, whole and entire, under each species. This means that after the Consecration, Christ is present whole and entire in each particle of each species. If the species are broken, Christ's body is not broken. It is whole in each part. If the species corrupt, Christ's Body does not corrupt; it simply ceases to be there any longer.

Christ gave power to his priests to change bread and wine into his Body and Blood when he said to his Apostles at the Last Supper, "Do this for a commemoration of me." The priests of God alone have this power, and they exercise it through the words: "This is my Body; this is my Blood." This power is part of the priestly character and is not lost even if a priest should unfortunately fall away and become heretical, schismatic, or be excommunicated. The priest, however, must have permission or jurisdiction from proper authority if he wishes to make a lawful use of his power of consecrating.

The bread used at Mass must be made of wheat flour. In the Latin rite, it is not fermented or salted, while in the Greek rite, it is fermented. The wine is the fermented juice of grapes. Although a priest may consecrate bread and wine anywhere and at any time, he may lawfully do so only when he offers Mass on an altar having a consecrated altar stone that is properly covered with altar cloths and corporal.

As regards the matter and form of this sacrament, the matter is wheaten bread and wine from the grape. The form is the words spoken over the bread: "This is my Body"; and over the wine: "This is my Blood."

The sacrament of the Eucharist is called by various names:

• *The Blessed Eucharist*, which means "holy Thanksgiving," because Jesus gave thanks to his Father at its institution, and also because we can offer him to God as our thanksgiving when he enters our souls in Holy Communion.

• *Holy Communion*, because when Jesus enters our souls in Holy Communion, we are united with him and made one with him.

• *The Blessed Sacrament*, because it is the holiest of all the sacraments.

• *The Sacrament of the Altar*, because Jesus remains reposed on the altar so that we may come and speak to him.

• *The Sacred Host*, because Jesus is offered up as the Host, or Victim, in the sacrifice of the Mass. This name is also given to the Sacred Hosts or pieces thereof.

• *Holy Viaticum*, which means "food for a journey." This is the name given to Holy Communion of the dying, because it is the food of the soul on its journey to eternity.

The dispositions necessary for a fruitful reception of the sacrament of the Holy Eucharist are to be in the state of sanctifying grace and to observe the prescribed fast beforehand.

The effects of Holy Communion are: 1) to unite us to Jesus and to nourish our soul with his divine life; 2) to increase sanctifying grace and all virtues in our soul; 3) to lessen our evil inclinations; 4) to be a pledge of everlasting life; 5) to fit our bodies for a glorious resurrection; and 6) to continue the sacrifice of the Cross in his Church.

The Blessed Eucharist was foreshown in prophetic types both in the Old Testament and in the New; it was promised expressly by Jesus one year before his death, after the feeding of the five thousand in the desert with five barley loaves and two fishes, shortly before the feast of Passover.[217] In the Old Testament, the manna in the desert prefigured the sacrament of the Holy Eucharist. The manna was bread that God sent from heaven to nourish the Israelites on their journey through the desert to the Promised Land.[218] The Blessed Eucharist is the True Bread from heaven, which nourishes our souls on our journey through this world to heaven, our Promised Land. The manna ceased to appear when the Israelites reached the Promised Land; the Blessed Eucharist will cease when we get to heaven.

In the New Testament, we read that Jesus multiplied bread so that with five small barley loaves, he fed five thousand, plus the women and children who were with them.[219] Each day, Jesus multiplies his sacred Body and gives himself to millions of souls all over the earth.

On the day after the feeding of the five thousand, when the people came searching for Jesus at Capernaum, he told them not to seek so earnestly for bodily food but to seek for the food of their souls. He said to them: "Labor not for the meat which perishes but for that which endures unto everlasting life, which the Son of

---

[217]John 6.
[218]Cf. Exod. 16:11-15.
[219]Matt. 14:15-21; Mark 6:35-44; Luke 9:12-17; John 6.

Man will give you . . . I am the living bread which came down from heaven. If any man eat of this bread, he shall live forever, and the bread that I shall give you is my Flesh for the life of the world . . . Unless you eat the Flesh of the Son of Man, and drink his Blood, you shall not have life in you . . . He that eats my Flesh and drinks my Blood has everlasting life, and I will raise him up on the last day. For my Flesh is meat indeed, and my Blood is drink indeed."[220]

The Blessed Sacrament is different from all the other sacraments, because it is a sacrament and a sacrifice. The other sacraments give us God's grace, but the Blessed Eucharist gives us God himself. The other sacraments pass away with the outward sign, although their effects remain in the soul; but the Blessed Eucharist is a permanent or lasting sacrament. Jesus remains as long as the appearances of bread and wine remain.

---

[220]Cf. Jn.6:27, 51-52, 54-56 (RSV = John 6:27, 51, 53-55).

Chapter 26

The Holy Eucharist as a Sacrifice

We observed in the previous chapter that, at the Last Supper, when Jesus changed the substance of bread and wine into his Body and Blood, he said to his Apostles: "Do this for a commemoration of me."[221] By these words he instituted the priesthood of the New Covenant, because he gave his Apostles power to do what he had done — that is, to change bread and wine into his Body and Blood, and then to offer him to the Father as he was about to offer himself in sacrifice on the morrow. The Apostles, in turn, transferred this power to others, and thus the power of the priesthood has continued in the Church, and will continue until the end of time. And one of the reasons Jesus instituted the sacrament of the Eucharist was to continue the sacrifice of the Cross in his Church.

The Holy Eucharist is a sacrament and a sacrifice. Holy Communion is the reception of the Holy Eucharist as a sacrament; the Mass is the Holy Eucharist in the character of a sacrifice. The Church defines the Mass as the unbloody sacrifice of the Body and Blood of Christ. The Mass is a real sacrifice in itself and also a re-presentation of the Sacrifice of the Cross. Here Jesus exercises his eternal priesthood and continually offers a clean oblation.[222]

[221]Luke 22:19.
[222]Ps. 109 (RSV = Ps. 110); Mal. 1:11.

The words of Consecration show that the Mass is a sacrifice. This is also indicated by the fact that it was celebrated right after the celebration of the paschal lamb, and just before the sacrifice of the Cross, and by the fact that Jesus used practically the same words that Moses used in his great sacrifice. At the consecration of the bread, the Gospel says that while they were at supper Jesus took bread, blessed and broke it, and gave it to his disciples and said: "Take and eat. This is my body." And taking the chalice, he gave thanks and gave it to them, saying: "Drink ye all of this. For this is my blood of the new testament, which shall be shed for many for the remission of sins."[223]

At the institution of the Old Covenant, Moses took the blood of the sacrificed animals and sprinkled it upon the people, and said: "This is the blood of the covenant which the Lord has made with you concerning all these words."[224]

Sacrifice is the highest act of worship. From the beginning of time, men have known that they must worship God by sacrifice. At first it was an instinct of the natural law, but afterward it was expressly commanded by God. In the Old Law, the Jewish people offered sheep, oxen, corn, and other things that support life. There were four types of sacrifices under the Mosaic Law: 1) holocausts, or whole burnt offerings, were the highest act of adoration; 2) eucharistic sacrifices, or thanksgiving offerings for favors received; 3) propitiation sacrifices, offered in atonement for sin; and 4) impetration sacrifices, offered to obtain new favors. In the New Law, we have one sacrifice, the Mass, offered for these same four ends. The sacrifices of the Old Covenant were pleasing to God only because they were figures or types of the great Sacrifice of his

[223]Matt. 26:26-28.
[224]Exod. 24:8.

divine Son, which he was to offer on the Cross, and which he continues to offer in each Mass.

Sacrifice consists in the offering of a victim, by a priest, to God alone, to acknowledge that he is our sovereign Lord. We offer an outward or visible sacrifice as a sign of the invisible offering of ourselves to God. The Mass is the same sacrifice as that of the Cross because in both the sacrifice of the Mass and in that of the Cross, there is the same Victim offered — namely, Jesus; and the same Priest who offers the sacrifice — Jesus.[225] And the ends for which the Mass is offered are the same as those for which the Sacrifice of the Cross was offered: to honor and glorify God; to thank him for all the graces he has bestowed on the whole world; to satisfy God's justice for the sins of men; and to obtain all graces and blessings. The Crucifixion was the noblest of prayers. This prayer is continued in the Mass.

About four hundred years before the time of Christ, the prophet Malachi foretold the offering of the Sacrifice of the Mass, saying: "From the rising of the sun to the going down, my name is great among the Gentiles, and in every place, there is sacrifice, and there is offered to my name a clean oblation, for my name is great among the Gentiles, said the Lord of hosts."[226] We know that Malachi referred to the Sacrifice of the Mass and not to that of the Cross, because the Sacrifice of the Cross was offered once only, and not continually, as the Mass is offered "from the rising to the setting of the sun."

Moreover, the Sacrifice of the Cross was offered only in one place — that is, on Mount Calvary — but the Mass is offered in all the countries of the world. In the Sacrifice of the Cross, there

---

[225]*Baltimore Catechism*, no. 3, 107.
[226]Mal. 1:11.

was an actual shedding of blood, and Jesus was really slain; but in the Mass, there is no shedding of blood nor real death, because Jesus can die no more; but in the Sacrifice of Mass, by means of the separate consecration of the bread and wine, his death on the Cross is re-presented.

As we have already said, Jesus commanded his Apostles and their successors to say Mass, when he said at the Last Supper: "Do this for a commemoration of me." The Last Supper was the first Mass ever said, and in it Holy Communion was given for the first time. The Apostles were the first to receive Holy Communion and at the same time were ordained priests. As, in the Old Testament, the Paschal Lamb was sacrificed in remembrance of the deliverance of the Chosen People from the slavery of Egypt, so in the New Testament, the Mass is offered in remembrance of our redemption from the slavery of sin.

Types of the Mass are the sacrifice of Abel, who offered to God the firstborn of his flock, in worship, as the eternal Father himself would later offer his only-begotten and well-beloved Son, "the first born of every creature" for the redemption of mankind.[227] The sacrifice of Isaac prepared by Abraham, his father, was a graphic symbol of the sacrifice of Jesus by the eternal Father for the redemption of Man. Melchisedek, who was king of Jerusalem and a priest of the most high God, offered a sacrifice of bread and wine in thanksgiving to God for Abraham's victory over the kings.[228] In his person, his office of high priest, and his kingship, he was a graphic symbol of Jesus, who continually offers himself to the eternal Father in the Sacrifice of the Mass, under the appearances of bread and wine.

[227]Cf. Col. 1:12-20.
[228]Cf. Gen. 14:18-20; Heb. 7:1-2.

The Mass does not redeem men. That was done on Calvary. But the Mass brings to men the fruits of redemption. The priest, the faithful assisting, and all the faithful of the Church share in the fruits of the Mass. The Mass is infinite in value and may be offered for many special intentions. We should assist at Mass with great interior recollection and piety, and with every mark of outward respect and devotion.

Because the Eucharist is such a profound mystery, many simply reject it and turn away. How can this be, they argue? How can Christ give us his Flesh to eat, or how can he abide beneath the appearances of bread and wine? These are the age-old questions that men have asked throughout the ages concerning the Real and abiding Presence of Jesus in the Holy Eucharist. They are an echo of the first objections that were raised by the multitude on the very day that Jesus promised to give himself to Man as the Bread of Life. "How can this man give us his flesh to eat?" they asked.[229] The question touches vitally upon the domain of faith. All such doubts essentially reveal a lack of faith. It is a question of the human mind preoccupying itself with a mystery, a work of God that is beyond its power to grasp, a work of divine omnipotence that transcends the powers of a finite mind to comprehend. For to assert or imply that God could not do such a thing is to deny that he is almighty. But if one admits that he is really almighty, then the logical conclusion to the problem is that he can literally do all things, as the angel Gabriel said to the Virgin Mary at the time of the Annunciation: "No word shall be impossible with God."[230]

The sacrament is a work of God's omnipotent power, goodness, and love, and although Man can never hope to comprehend it,

---

[229]John 6:53 (RSV = John 6:52).
[230]Luke 1:37.

God has enabled him at least to accept it, by a guarantee of his unlimited power of action as manifested in this visible creation. When we behold the vast and profound natural mystery that surrounds us in the universe, how can we doubt that the Author of such a complex and unfathomable creation is capable of greater wonders on a spiritual plane?

Chapter 27

The Institutional Church Today

In this time of shifting values, when the most honored traditions of antiquity are being called into question, the Church in her most venerable structures and doctrines is violently assailed. The decisions and teachings of the Magisterium are questioned, debated, challenged, and very often summarily rejected. Indeed it would seem that in order to become popular, one must find fault with the institutional Church. Such unwarranted assault, especially on the part of religious, betrays not only an ignorance of Christian history, but also a basic lack of faith in the divine origin of the Church.

Among the most important censures brought against the Institutional Church today, sometimes even by religious, is its very structure. It is too highly structured, they say, too functional in its approach, too much of a bureaucracy, and as such, cannot be accepted by today's society. Moreover, the Church exercises her authority in a high-handed and arrogant manner, like the rule of an absolute monarch in former ages; but the days of despotism and dictatorship are ended, and people will no longer stand for such a type of rule.

These sweeping assertions might be impressive, but they cannot stand up to the light of rational investigation. To begin with, no one can deny that the Church is a highly structured institution, but its structure grew out of necessity, by a natural process of development, the result of existing circumstances, as the structure of any institution in secular society develops. In the beginning there was no need for such complex structure as that which exists today, because the Church was confined to a very circumscribed region, within a small geographical area. But as time went on, it began to expand and was thus compelled by necessity to institute various governmental structures, to preserve order, to ensure union with the central authority at Rome, and above all, to preserve the integrity of the Faith.

Yet the Church cannot be compared to any secular form of government, either in her structure or her function, because she is unique in her nature and office. In certain aspects she may re-semble a monarchy, a republic, or even a democracy, but at a cer-tain point she ceases to resemble any natural type and becomes unique in herself, as the kingdom of God on earth, whose archi-tect is Christ.[231] He rules through his Vicar, the Supreme Pontiff, and Shepherd of his flock, who is the Bishop of Rome. Jesus had a great deal to say about the way in which his vicar and the other shepherds of his Church were to exercise their authority.

He said to them: "You know that the princes of the Gentiles lord it over them, and they that are the greater exercise power upon them. It shall not be so among you; but whosoever will be the greater among you, let him be your minister, and he that will be first among you shall be your servant, even as the Son of Man is not come to be ministered unto, but to minister, and to give his life a redemption for many."[232] At the Last Supper, he washed his Apostles' feet to signify the manner in which they were to go about the work of winning the world to the gospel. They were not

---

[231]Cf. Heb. 2:1-14.
[232]Matt. 20:25-28.

to lord it over men but to exercise their authority in a spirit of lowly service.

But Christ had also much to say about the obedience and respect required of those who accepted the gospel and chose to become his disciples. For the obedience and respect accorded to those whom he had charged to preach the gospel in his name, he took as given to himself. He said: "He who receives you receives me, and he who receives me receives him that sent me. He that hears you hears me, and he that despises you despises me, and he that despises me despises him that sent me."[233] It is evident, therefore, that the Church cannot exercise her authority in a highhanded or arbitrary manner if she is to be faithful to the mandate of Christ.

Now it is precisely this divinely bestowed authority with which we are confronted when dealing with the grave issues that trouble society today, whether they be moral issues or those pertaining to ministries within the Church. Whatever their nature, they are of first-rate importance and have vast and profound implications not only for the Church herself but for the entire human family. Often the rage and storm that revolve around these issues spring from a mistaken idea that the Church is acting through arrogance, yet nothing could be further from the truth. For the issues in question are too serious and far-reaching in their implications to allow of their being settled by the caprice of human emotion. In this matter, the Church is very conscious of the nature of her authority and of her mandate to exercise it in the defense of truth.

The words of Jesus to Pilate are directly applicable here: "For this was I born, and for this I came into the world, that I should give testimony to the truth. Everyone who is of the truth listens to

[233]Matt. 10:40; Luke 10:16.

my voice."[234] His voice still speaks through the Church, which he has constituted the teacher and guardian of truth. Sometimes it is more convenient to say that two and two make five, but that does not alter the fact that two and two always make four.

In dealing with these issues, the Church must stand firm as a rock and proclaim that evil is evil, and wrong is wrong; but this she does calmly, and uninfluenced by passion, with genuine compassion for those who are blind to the truth or who have been led astray by the false philosophies of the day. And for those who storm against her teaching, whether within or outside the Catholic fold, they will inevitably discover that it is easy to accept decisions, once convinced that there is no personal enmity behind the legislation of the Magisterium, only fidelity to the mandate of Christ.

Another complaint and cause of grave concern to religious today is the scandal to be found within the Church, often within the ranks of the religious life itself. This poses a serious problem to the work of the gospel and is a perennial cause of offense to those outside the household of the Catholic Faith, for it brings the Church into the contempt of her enemies. "Who could believe or abide in such a Church," they say, "much less look upon her as holy?" Certainly this is true, but it is not the complete truth.

First of all, we must admit that these scandals exist within the Church, and who would want to deny it? But then, Jesus, in founding the Church, was well aware that such would be the case, and if we might say so with reverence, he made provision for such a possibility. For within the apostolic college, which was the Church's basic foundation, he permitted that scandal should be found. In his supreme hour of need, Judas, one of his chosen Twelve, betrayed

[234]John 18:37.

him to death, and Peter, the one upon whom he had promised to build his Church, swore that he never knew Jesus.

In regard to scandal, he had much to say, however, for he was well aware of its intrinsic evil and devastating effects. St. Matthew records what he said in regard to scandal to children: "He that shall scandalize one of these little ones that believe in me, it were better for him that a millstone should be hanged about his neck and that he should be drowned in the depth of the sea. Woe to the world because of scandals. For it must needs be that scandals come but nevertheless woe to that man by whom the scandal comes."[235] "Children" meant not only the very young but also the simple faithful.

When we come to consider scandal more closely, however, we find certain factors that may help to relieve the darkness. First, we should realize that beneath this regrettable evil, we are all of the family of Christ, and when one offends, it reflects upon the whole family. Such tragic failures cause a deep sense of embarrassment to many of the faithful, as the members of a natural family might feel at the disgrace of one of its own, but still they will try to shield the guilty one from public scorn, while deploring his wrongdoing.

In the same way, the religious family should try to shield the fallen brother or sister from public contempt, while deploring the wrong, because it is well to remember that they fell, not because they were Catholic, or religious, but because they were the fallen children of Adam, and such a tragedy could have befallen anyone. It was to this that St. Paul alluded when he said: "Let him who stands take heed lest he fall"; "we have this treasure in earthen vessels"; "be not high-minded but fear."[236] We see only the fall, not

[235]Matt. 18:6-7.
[236]1 Cor. 10:12; 2 Cor. 4:7; Rom. 11:20.

the brave struggle to stand firm in the face of temptation, which might have preceded it. And if ultimately they failed in the contest, who can condemn?

It is likewise well to remember, too, that while the world may scoff, the fallen brother or sister may feel deep remorse for their failure, even though they might never reveal their personal feelings to the public, and this deep hurt might continue long after the world has forgotten. Scathing criticism accomplishes nothing: it merely adds to that hidden pain. Rather, it is silence born of charity that in the end proves far more effective in helping to heal the moral evil of scandal than decrying it from the housetops.

Such simple reflections are usually sufficient to bring those scandalized to a kinder way of thinking; but there are still the few who say that because of such scandals within her ranks, the Church has no right to presume to teach others, and should be forbidden to do so. Perhaps this difficulty might be resolved by a comparison with secular governments. There is no secular government on earth that is wholly free from corruption, but the fact that such is the case in no way detracts from the excellence of the idea of a well-organized system of government. It would be tragic, therefore, to destroy the idea, because of the failure of a few.

It is the same with the Church, which is a divine institution, but composed of frail and fallible human persons, the fallen children of Adam. It is because of their human frailty that the institution sometimes became corrupt in the past, but that was not the defect of the institution but rather of the fallible agents who governed it. Yet it is precisely through the weakness and defect of these imperfect instruments that God works to accomplish his designs. If everyone and everything were perfect within the Church, people would not be surprised, because it would be only what they expected, but for God to achieve the great designs of his glory with such imperfect instruments is a source of never-ending astonishment to all who behold it. Indeed when we contemplate the history of the Church through the ages, with its shining peaks of glory on the one hand, and its dark shadows on the other, we are led to exclaim with St. Paul: "O the depth of the riches of the wisdom and of the knowledge of God! How incomprehensible are his judgments and how unsearchable his ways! For who has known the mind of the Lord or who has been his counselor? For of him, and by him, and in him, are all things: to him be glory forever. Amen."[237]

[237]Rom. 11:33-36.

Part 5

The Seventh Day:
The Last Things

Chapter 28

The End of the World

In the foregoing chapters of this work, we have considered the pilgrimage of Man through the ages, from the days of Eden to the present day. Now it is time to ask ourselves when and where this pilgrimage will end. This question concerns not only mankind as a whole, but each individual of the human family, and it is only from divine revelation that we can obtain an answer. For even in this nuclear and space age, science can give no certain facts about the completion of the human destiny. It can speculate to a certain degree, but all speculation in this matter is, in the end, only human opinion. To find the facts, we must turn to Christ.

Jesus alone could look into the distant future and give an eyewitness account of when and how this pilgrimage of Man through time will come to an end. What he has told us, he has told us as God, and it is therefore sure, reliable, and complete, stark and terrifying in its content, yet calm and sober in its certainty.

The subject of the consummation of Man's earthly destiny was first broached by the Apostles, very shortly before Jesus' Passion, after he had come out of the Temple and was sitting on the slopes of Mount Olivet, opposite this glorious building. Taking advantage of this respite, they asked him about the end of the world. They opened their conversation with a casual remark about the beauty of the Temple opposite them, which was still under reconstruction long after the death of Herod the Great, who had begun it more than twenty years before. "Master," they said to him, with a touch of pride, "behold what manner of stones and what buildings are here." Jesus replied: "Do you see all these great buildings? There shall not be left a stone upon a stone that shall not be thrown down." Certainly they were not expecting such a reply, for it was unthinkable that any such horrendous misfortune should come to pass, so they instantly took up his remark and said to him: "Tell us when shall these things be, and what shall be the sign of thy coming and of the consummation of the world?"[238]

It was then that Jesus launched into an account of what shall happen at the end of the world. We have to read all four Gospels to get a fair sketch of this cosmic event.

Jesus said in part:

> When you shall hear of wars and rumors of wars, do not fear. For such things must needs be, but the end is not yet. For nation shall rise against nation and kingdom against kingdom; and there shall be pestilences and famines and earthquakes in places. Now, all these things are the beginnings of sorrows.
>
> And there shall be signs in the sun and in the moon and in the stars; and upon the earth distress of nations, by reason of the confusion of the roaring of the sea and of the waves; men withering away for fear and expectation of what shall come upon the whole world. And many false prophets shall arise and shall seduce many. And because iniquity has abounded, the charity of many shall grow cold.
>
> But he that shall persevere to the end, he shall be saved. And this gospel of the kingdom shall be preached in the

[238]Matt. 24:1-3; Mark 13:1-4.

whole world, for a testimony to all nations; and then shall the consummation come.[239]

He spoke at great length of various other signs and events that shall precede his Second Coming. His discourse could be summed up in his own words:

There shall be then great tribulation, such as has not been from the beginning of the world until now, neither shall be. And unless those days had been shortened, no flesh should be saved; but for the sake of the elect, those days shall be shortened.

And immediately after the tribulation of those days, the sun shall be darkened and the moon shall not give her light, and the stars shall fall from heaven, and the powers of heaven shall be moved. And then shall appear the sign of the Son of Man in heaven. And then shall all the tribes of the earth mourn; and they shall see the Son of Man coming in the clouds of heaven with much power and majesty. And he shall send his angels with a trumpet and a great voice; and they shall gather together his elect from the four winds, from the farthest parts of the heavens to the utmost bounds of them. And from the fig tree learn a parable: when the branch thereof is now tender and the leaves come forth, you know that summer is nigh. So you also, when you see all these things, know that it is nigh, even at the doors. Heaven and earth shall pass: but my words shall not pass.

What exactly did these predictions mean to the people who heard them from the lips of Jesus, either directly or through the

[239]Luke 21:25-26; Matt. 24:14.

apostles? At that time, probably about eighty percent of the human race were ignorant of the physical constitution of the universe and the laws that governed it. The average person was totally unconcerned about such matters. That the sun could be darkened would seem impossible, and since the moon receives its light from the sun, it, too, would be plunged in darkness. That the stars should fall from the heavens was just too much to take, for the ordinary person who looked upon the whole creation as eternally stable and whole.

Throughout the centuries, many have speculated on when the Second Coming shall be, but Jesus tells us:

> Of that day and hour no one knows; no, not the angels of heaven, but the Father alone. And as in the days of Noah, so shall also the coming of the Son of Man be. For, as in the days before the flood, they were eating and drinking, marrying and giving in marriage, even till that day in which Noah entered into the ark, and they knew not till the flood came and took them all away, so also shall the coming of the Son of Man be. Then two shall be in the field. One shall be taken, and one shall be left. Two women shall be grinding at the mill. One shall be taken, and one shall be left.
>
> Watch, therefore, because you know not what hour your Lord will come. For as lightning comes out of the east and appears even into the west, so shall also the coming of the Son of Man be. Wheresoever the body shall be, there shall the eagles also be gathered together.

St. Peter adds:

> In those days there shall come deceitful scoffers, saying: Where is his promise or his coming? For since the time that

the fathers slept, all things continue as they were from the beginning of the creation . . . But of this one thing be not ignorant, my beloved, that one day with the Lord is as a thousand years, and a thousand years as one day. The Lord does not delay his promise, as some imagine, but deals patiently for your sake, not willing that any should perish, but that all should return to penance.

But the day of the Lord shall come as a thief, in which the heavens shall pass away with great violence, and the elements shall be melted with heat, and the earth and the works which are in it shall be burnt up.

As we can see, it is not ours to know when Christ will return. But we know that when he does, the world will have been carrying on as normal, and then in a flash, the universe will begin to disintegrate. Therefore, we should always bear in mind Jesus' final warning:

Watch . . . for you do not know when the Lord of the house is coming, at evening or at midnight, or at the cockcrowing, or in the morning. Lest coming on a sudden, he find you sleeping. And what I say to you, I say to all: Watch.

Jesus clearly indicated that he was coming to judge all mankind in a great and final judgment. About five centuries previously, during the Babylonian Captivity, the prophet Daniel was given a vision of that awesome event. He said:

I beheld till thrones were placed and the Ancient of Days sat. His garment was white as snow and the hair of his head like clean wool; his throne like flames of fire; the wheels of it like a burning fire. A swift stream of fire issued forth from before him; thousands of thousands ministered to him, and ten thousand times a hundred thousand [one billion] stood before him. The judgment sat and the books were opened . . .

I beheld therefore in the vision of the night, and lo, one like the Son of Man came with the clouds of heaven. And he came even to the Ancient of days; and they presented him before him. And he gave him power and glory and a kingdom; and all peoples, tribes and tongues shall serve him. His power is an everlasting power that shall not be taken away; and his kingdom that shall not be destroyed.

Finally, Jesus spoke to the apostle John, in the book of Revelation of the mystery of his Second Coming as judge of mankind. He said:

Behold, he comes with the clouds, and every eye shall see him; and they also that pierced him. And all the tribes of the earth shall bewail themselves because of him. Even so, Amen. I am Alpha and Omega, the beginning and the end, says the Lord God, who is and who was and who is to come, the Almighty.

Let us now speak briefly about the Last Judgment.

Chapter 29

The General Judgment

In its formal teaching of the great dogmas of the Christian Faith, the Apostles' Creed says of Jesus: "He suffered under Pontius Pilate, was crucified, died, and was buried. The third day he rose again from the dead. He ascended into heaven and is seated at the right hand of God, the Father almighty. From thence he shall come to judge the living and the dead."

Jesus spoke very clearly and at length about his return at the end of the world to judge the living and the dead, as we have seen in the last chapter, and he also spoke at length about the actual Judgment itself, which is recorded in the twenty-fifth chapter of St. Matthew's Gospel. It will be of interest, therefore, to consider this important dogma of the Faith. But before doing so, it might be helpful to reflect briefly upon what the Church teaches about the final destiny of Man.

The closing of his earthly destiny is usually referred to as the four last things — namely, death, judgment, heaven, and hell. It is from Scripture itself that the Church learns this. The book of Genesis says: "God created Man from the slime of the earth and breathed into his face the breath of life, and Man became a living soul."[240] The body of Man, therefore, was made of matter, but each soul is a special creation of God. When Man dies, his body returns

[240]Gen. 2:7.

to dust, but the soul lives on because it cannot die. It is a living, intelligent being. God himself, the good and bad angels, and the souls of men are the only spirits in existence.

The body can return to dust — that is, to its component parts — but the soul, being a spirit — and being like to God in that it has understanding and free will — has no component parts and therefore cannot die. It continues to live on, even when it has separated from the body. We first come face-to-face with this mystery of death in Sacred Scripture when it records the trial and the Fall of Man in the Garden of Eden, or the Garden of Paradise, immediately after his creation. The scriptural account says: "And the Lord God took Man, and put him in the paradise of pleasure, to dress it, and to keep it. And he commanded him saying: 'Of every tree of paradise you shall eat. But of the Tree of Knowledge of Good and Evil, you shall not eat. For in what day soever you shall eat of it, you shall die the death.' "[241]

The Church says that this trial was willed by God to try Man's obedience, and his willingness to acknowledge God's sovereign authority as the one from whom he had received all good. But Man failed in the test and ate the forbidden fruit; as a result, he lost the wonderful hierarchy of gifts with which God endowed him at his creation, and he became estranged from his Supreme benefactor and friend. Among the gifts he lost was that of immortality of the body. He became subject to illness and death, and indeed he felt the effects of this withdrawal of grace in every part of his being. The Church sums up the result of Man's sin when she says that his Fall from grace darkened his understanding, weakened his will, and left in him a strong inclination toward evil. This first sin of Man is called Original Sin, that is, the first sin.

[241]Gen. 2:15-17.

The malice of that first sin did not lie in the actual eating of the fruit, but rather, in the pride of mind that led Adam to disobey God's command. He was not satisfied to be simply the son or friend of God; he wanted to be equal to God. In punishment for his disobedience, God passed sentence upon him, and upon those who were involved with him in the transgression of the divine command.

He said to Adam: "Because you have hearkened to the voice of your wife, and have eaten of the tree whereof I commanded you that you should not eat, cursed is the earth in your work; with labor and toil shall you eat thereof all the days of your life. Thorns and thistles shall it bring forth to you; and you shall eat the herbs of the earth. In the sweat of your face shall you eat bread till you return to the earth out of which you were taken: for dust you are, and into dust you shall return."[242] This was God's first judgment upon Man, at the very dawn of human history, a sentence of condemnation, but it was not without hope, for in passing judgment upon the serpent, he showed clearly that he had forgiven Man and, in time, would redeem him from the consequences of his sin, by sending him a Savior. He said to the serpent: "I will put enmity between you and the woman, and your seed and her seed; she shall crush your head, and you shall lie in wait for her heel."[243]

In that sentence of judgment upon the serpent, which the Church says was actually the Devil, God signified the forgiveness of Man's sin and the promise of a Redeemer. Man would discover later that this Promised Redeemer was none other than God's only-begotten and well-beloved Son, Jesus.

But after the Fall, Man's nature was no longer perfect or whole. He suffered from the effects of his sin in every part of his being;

[242]Gen. 3:17-19.
[243]Gen. 3:15.

and it was in this imperfect state that he was to try to serve God, until the Redeemer should come. When Jesus came, he revealed to mankind that he indeed was the Promised Savior. He said of himself:

I am the good shepherd; I know mine, and mine know me. The good shepherd gives his life for his sheep. And other sheep I have that are not of this fold. Them also I must bring. And they shall hear my voice, and there shall be one fold and one shepherd.

Therefore does the Father love me, because I lay down my life, that I may take it again. No man takes it away from me, but I lay it down of myself. And I have power to lay it down, and I have power to take it up again. This commandment I have received of my Father. And as the Father has given me commandments, so do I.

Unless the grain of wheat falling into the ground die, itself remains alone. But if it die, it brings forth much fruit. And I, if I be lifted up from the earth, will draw all things to myself. (Now this he said, signifying what death he should die.) I have come that they may have life and may have it more abundantly. Behold, I make all things new."[244]

St. Peter, when addressing the religious authorities, shortly after Pentecost, said of Jesus: "This is the stone which was rejected by you the builders, which is become the head of the corner. Neither is there salvation in any other. For there is no other name under heaven given to men, whereby we must be saved."[245]

---

[244]John 10:14, 16-18; 14:31; 12:24-25, 32-33; 10:10; Apoc. 21:5 (RSV = Rev. 21:5).
[245]Acts 4:11-12.

So God would redeem his fallen child, but Man would none-theless be expected to cooperate in the work of redemption by showing his love and respect for God and living by his Law, whether the Natural or the Mosaic Law. Moreover, he was to live with a sense of responsibility or accountability, to use his talents to glorify his Divine Majesty. We know this from the parables of the Ten Virgins,[246] the talents,[247] the unjust steward,[248] and Dives and Lazarus.[249] It will be upon his use or neglect of his talents in the ser-vice of his fellowman that Man will be judged at the Second Com-ing of Christ.

[246]Matt. 25:1-13.
[247]Matt. 25:14-30.
[248]Luke 16:1-9.
[249]Luke 16:19-31.

Chapter 30

The Particular Judgment

The General Judgment of all mankind will occur at the Second Coming; it will be the Last and Final Judgment. But meanwhile, God will call every individual to a personal account of his life immediately after death. This is called the Particular Judgment,[250] and it will determine whether he will be saved or lost forever; it cannot be reversed. It might well be asked, then, why, if a person is judged immediately after death, will there be need of a General Judgment? The Church says that there is need of a General Judgment so that the providence of God, which on earth often permits the good to suffer and the wicked to prosper, may in the end appear just before all men.[251]

There are many questions Man has been asking since the dawn of time that seem to defy explanation in this life. Who, for example, can explain the deep hurt and pain of life that surround us on every side today, despite the advanced technology and the many comforts of life that were unknown to former generations? Who can explain the loneliness of heart, or the unfulfilled desire for happiness that ever seems to elude Man's grasp, even when he is surrounded by the good things of life? How can we account for the

[250]*Baltimore Catechism*, no. 3, 161; cf. CCC, 266.

[251]*Baltimore Catechism*, no. 3, 162; for an in-depth reading, cf. CCC, 272.

broken hearts and broken lives we encounter every day, even among those who live in luxury?

The General Judgment will answer these questions, but only insofar as God wills it, for in his hidden counsels, there may be many questions he will choose to leave unanswered, even in eternal life. St. Paul touched upon this mystery when he said: "Who has known the mind of the Lord? Or who has been his counselor?"[252] One thing is certain, however: all the hurts and pains of life as we know it here on earth will be removed by God before we enter the kingdom of heaven. All wrongs will be righted, and all justice will be restored to perfect balance, and our everlasting life in heaven will be whole and perfect in its happiness and peace."[253]

But let us return for a moment to the question of death. What happens to Man immediately after death? Here we come to the four last things: death, judgment, heaven, and hell. The Church says that at death the soul will be judged with strict justice according to its deeds.[254] The rewards or punishments appointed for the souls of men, therefore, are heaven, purgatory, or hell.

The Church defines heaven as a state of everlasting life in which we see God face-to-face, are made like to him in glory, and enjoy eternal happiness. St. Paul says, when speaking of heaven, that "eye has not seen, nor ear heard, neither has it entered into the heart of Man what things God has prepared for them that love him."[255]

It is not an easy thing to enter heaven immediately after death, for the Church says that nothing defiled can enter heaven.[256] Before

---

[252]Rom. 11:34.
[253]Cf. Apoc. 21 (RSV = Rev. 21).
[254]Matt. 16:27.
[255]1 Cor. 2:9.
[256]Apoc. 21:27 (RSV = Rev. 21:27).

one can enter heaven, the home of God, all mortal or venial sin must be remitted, and the temporal punishment due to sin must also have been removed, so that no stain of sin may mar the beauty of the soul that is destined to stand before God and abide in his home for all eternity. In a word, the soul must die in the love of God, and at peace with him. We shall have more to say about heaven in the following chapters.

However, we need to clarify a certain point about the entrance of the soul into heaven. While God requires that each and every soul be spotlessly clean in order to enter the home of eternal happiness, what will become of those who die in the friendship of God, but are still not perfectly holy? They are not bad enough to deserve hell, nor yet good enough to enter heaven. Here again it is from the revelation of Christ that we must find the answer.

From the deposit of divine revelation, the Church teaches that those who die with venial — that is, lesser — sins on their soul, or without having satisfied for the temporal punishment due to sin, will be sent to a place of purgation or cleansing, which is called purgatory, until the last traces of sin are purged away. Jesus clearly revealed that this place of cleansing exists, and that moreover, sins will be forgiven in the next world.[257] There are some outside the fold of the Church who do not believe in purgatory and thus deprive themselves of a great hope and consolation.

Lastly we come to the question of hell. The Church defines hell as a state to which the wicked are condemned, in which they are deprived of the sight of God for all eternity and are in dreadful torments. Jesus clearly spoke about the existence of hell, as a very definite reality,[258] so that whether we accept or reject it, hell exists.

[257]Cf. Matt. 12:30-32.
[258]Cf. Matt. 5:29-30; 18:6-9.

Besides, there is a very clear account of the origin of hell in the book of Revelation, which says:

> There was a great battle in heaven: Michael and his angels fought with the dragon, and the dragon fought, and his angels. And they did not prevail; neither was their place found anymore in heaven. And that great dragon was cast out, that old serpent, who is called the Devil, and Satan, who seduces the whole world. And he was cast unto the earth; and his angels were thrown down with him. And I heard a loud voice in heaven, saying: Now is come salvation and strength, and the kingdom of our God and the power of his Christ, because the accuser of our brethren is cast forth, who accused them before our God day and night.
>
> And they overcame him by the blood of the Lamb and by the word of their testimony: and they loved not their lives unto death. Therefore, rejoice, O heavens, and you that dwell therein. Woe to the earth and to the sea, because the Devil is come down unto you, having great wrath, knowing that he has but a short time.[259]

But despite this clear revelation of Christ and of Sacred Scripture, there are many who scoff at the very idea of hell. They say that God cannot punish sin in that manner on account of his mercy; yet Scripture itself shows that God has always punished sin severely, as, for example, in the Great Deluge or the destruction of Sodom and Gomorrah. And when describing the Last Judgment, he said to those condemned: "Depart from me, you cursed, into everlasting fire, which was prepared for the Devil and his angels."[260]

[259] Apoc. 12:7-12 (RSV = Rev. 12:7-12).
[260] Matt. 25:41.

Others deny that hell is eternal and thus make of it a purgatory;[261] and perhaps the most fearful mistake of all is to say that some people are predestined (appointed beforehand) from birth, for heaven or hell. This is to proclaim that God is unjust or evil, besides the denial of free will to the individual to choose salvation or damnation. Such a belief would destroy all desire to serve God and would lead to despair. For why should one try to lead a good and holy life if, in the end, he was destined for hell anyway?

But if the soul turns away from God, and refuses to have any part with him, what remains but to consign him to eternal damnation? It has been well said that if such a one were to be forced into heaven, then heaven itself would become hell for that soul.

In treating of hell or eternal damnation, there is one consolation that offsets the terrifying reality of such a final tragedy, and that is the fathomless depths of the love of the eternal Father for every soul he has created. God will never condemn any soul to hell if there is even the slightest hope of repentance on the part of the one to be condemned. We know this from the revelation of Jesus throughout the Gospels, as, for example, in the parables of the Lost Sheep and the Prodigal Son.[262] It is wonderfully expressed also in the words God spoke through the prophet Isaiah: "Though your sins be as scarlet, they shall be made as white as snow."[263]

It is time now to give a final look at the closing of the book of human destiny.

---

[261] *Baltimore Catechism*, no. 3, 161. For in-depth reading, see CCC, 268 ff.

[262] Luke 15:3-10; 11-32.

[263] Isa. 1:18.

Chapter 31

The Closing of the Book of Human Destiny

In his description of the Last Judgment of Mankind, Jesus was very explicit. He said:

> When the Son of Man shall come in his majesty, and all the angels with him, then shall he sit upon the seat of his majesty. And all the nations shall be gathered together before him; and he shall separate them one from another, as the shepherd separates the sheep from the goats. And he shall set the sheep on his right hand, but the goats on his left. Then shall the King say to them that shall be on his right hand: "Come ye blessed of my Father, possess the kingdom prepared for you from the foundation of the world. For I was hungry and you gave me to eat; I was thirsty and you gave me to drink; I was a stranger and you took me in . . ." Then shall the just answer him, saying: "Lord when did we see you hungry and fed you; thirsty and gave you drink . . . ?" And the King answering shall say to them: "Amen, I say to you, as long as you did it to one of these my least brethren, you did it to me."
>
> Then he shall say to them also that shall be on his left hand: "Depart from me, you cursed, into everlasting fire, which was prepared for the Devil and his angels. For I was hungry and you gave me not to eat; I was thirsty and you

gave me not to drink . . ." Then they also shall answer him saying: "Lord, when did we see you hungry or thirsty or a stranger . . . and did not minister to you?" Then he shall answer them, saying: "Amen, I say to you, as long as you did it not to one of those least, neither did you do it to me." And these shall go everlasting punishment: but the just, into life everlasting.[264]

With this formal sentence the age-old pilgrimage of Man through time will close forever. The Church says that the bodies of the just will rise glorious and immortal. After the resurrection we shall have the same bodies, but they will be beautiful in proportion to the beauty of the soul.[265] The bodies of the just will be without any defect. They will be impassable — that is, not subject to suffering — glorious like the sun, swift as thought, and subtle or spiritual — that is, capable of penetrating matter.

The bodies of the damned will also rise, but they will be condemned to eternal punishment. There will be no beauty in the bodies of the damned on the day of General Judgment.

Immediately after the Judgment, mankind, under the leadership of Jesus, will step across the frontiers of time to enter the realm of eternity. When we think upon this awesome reality, we cannot but think of the serious nature of our life here on earth. The thoughts it naturally evokes are summed up in this beautiful poem.

> *Only one life is mine,*
> *One death its close,*
> *When shall that hour be?*
> *Only God knows.*

[264]Matt. 25:31-46.
[265]Rom. 8:11.

Only one soul is mine,
Endless its life,
Heaven or hell its home,
After the strife.

Only One eye sees all,
One judge of Man.
Earth's judgments pass away,
God's never can.

One life, one death, one soul,
Eternity . . .
All saved or lost forever,
Which shall it be?

Thomas à Kempis Reilly, O.P.
(1879-1957)

Now let us look at what lies beyond the frontier of time, in eternal life.

Chapter 32

The Eternal Sabbath

What is heaven? From the deposit of divine revelation, and most especially from the teaching of Christ, the Church defines heaven as a state of everlasting life in which we see God face-to-face, are made like unto Him in glory, and enjoy eternal happiness.[266] St. Paul, after having received a vision of heaven said: "Eye has not seen nor ear heard; neither has it entered into the heart of Man what things God has prepared for those that love him."[267]

The very idea of this afterlife brings many questions to mind, questions that, subconsciously at least, might fill us with a sense of apprehension rather than happiness. In dealing with these questions, we are moving on very unfamiliar ground, in a new dimension, so to speak, trying to explain the mysteries of eternity in the language of time. Yet in our endeavor, we may be greatly aided by the things of time, because this whole created universe is like a sign that points to a spiritual reality beyond itself. The various aspects of creation, therefore, dimly reflect the mysteries of eternal life.

The Church says that heaven is both a place and a state. The New Testament, for instance, frequently refers to heaven as a

---

[266]*Baltimore Catechism*, no. 3, 163. For further reading, see CCC, 267 ff. For in-depth reading on heaven, cf. E. J. Fortman, S.J., *Everlasting Life After Death* (New York: Alba House, 1976), 184 ff.

[267]1 Cor. 2:9.

place. Thus, St. Matthew, when recording the Baptism of Jesus, says that "the heavens were opened to him; and he saw the Spirit of God descending as a dove and coming upon him."[268] And in the Acts of the Apostles, we read that while the apostles were actually watching Jesus ascending into heaven, two men (angels) stood by them in white garments, who said to them: "Ye men of Galilee, why do you stand looking up to heaven? This Jesus who is taken up from you into heaven shall so come as you have seen him going into heaven."[269] Finally we have the statement in the Apostles' Creed: "He ascended into heaven and sits at the right hand of God, the Father Almighty; from thence he shall come to judge the living and the dead."

So, to repeat our definition, we can say that heaven is the home of God, where he abides in a very special manner and manifests his glory to the blessed, the home of everlasting happiness, to which we usually refer when we use the word *heaven*.

Another question that naturally comes to mind, and which may cause a sense of apprehension, is: What exactly does the Church mean by *eternal life*? Anything that is eternal, even in heaven, can, in a way, inspire a sense of dread, for the idea of eternity as "time without end" or "forever and ever" can be very formidable. Subconsciously we tend to regard anything that involves motion or activity as interesting or absorbing, and anything that denotes stillness or immobility as dull or boring. In a sense, therefore, time seems more appealing than eternity, for essentially it involves motion; indeed, it is philosophically defined as "the measure of motion." Being creatures of time, we are naturally attuned to the rhythm of constant motion.

[268]Matt. 3:16.
[269]Acts 1:10-11.

Eternity, on the contrary, is utterly opposed to time, for whereas time, in a sense, may be said to be composed of parts — namely, past, present, and future — eternity is an ever-present *now*. We could express it in another way by saying that in eternity there is no difference between our past, present, and future, for eternity embraces all time within itself. There is no goal to which we can walk in eternity, as we do in time, no goal for which we can strive, for we have already attained it; there is nothing more to wish for, for we possess all that we desire to achieve. Is it boredom, then, simply to be in heaven with nothing to "do"?

Certainly if our existence in heaven meant eternal inactivity, it would be eternal boredom, but who would dare assert that such is the case? Not everything that appears to be inactivity is necessarily so, and here we have our first example of how the material universe reflects the mystery of eternity. When we look at the starlit firmament with unaided vision, it seems so still, always the same, apparently unchangeable and immutable. But we know that beneath this exterior aspect of changelessness, there is constant dynamic and profound activity, so mysterious in its nature and dimension that it absorbs the interest, and challenges all the intellectual powers of the masterminds of science today. Exploring the activity of this apparently inactive creation, they find themselves immersed in a fathomless ocean of natural mystery whose depths they can never hope to sound.

Turning to the mystery of eternal life, we find the same thing in the supernatural order. The stillness or timelessness of eternity does not connote inactivity, but rather, the contrary. The activity of Man during the endless ages of eternity is much like that of the nuclear and space-age scientists of today, only far more vast and profound. For in eternity, Man will not be concerned with exploring the material universe, which, after all, is only an "effect," but rather, with sounding the depths of the mystery of God, who is the principle and first cause of this effect.

Now, if the study of the universe, which is only an effect of this Cause, can so absorb and delight Man that he is beside himself with wonder, what shall be his delight and wonder when confronted with the root cause of this effect?

Such wonder and delight can leave no room for boredom, for it will provide Man with the most intensely absorbing and fascinating activity we can imagine, and that for all eternity. Jesus himself touched upon this mysterious activity of the blessed in heaven in His prayer to the Father after the Last Supper, when He said: "Now, this is eternal life, that they may know thee, the only true God, and Jesus Christ, whom thou hast sent."[270] The essential happiness of heaven, therefore, will consist in the intellectual activity of the soul, as it tries to sound the unfathomable mystery of God, throughout the endless ages of eternity; yet eternity itself will never see an end to its quest.

To have some idea of the real delight and unfading happiness that this intellectual activity of the soul will afford to Man, we have only to look at its counterpart on earth. When the mind is engaged on intellectual pursuit, the heart is at rest. To be convinced of this, we have only to look at the astronomer in his observatory, the scientist in his laboratory, or the composer at work on his symphony. When Man is mentally absorbed, he is unaware of the passage of time. Indeed, this explains why even here on earth, where everything is tainted with imperfection, there is still, in this mortal existence, much to delight the heart of Man and make him loath to leave it. Let us examine a little more carefully the nature of this mysterious activity.

[270]John 17:3.

Chapter 33

The Mystery of Eternal Life

What exactly does the Church teach about the unveiled vision of God that will be granted to Man in heaven, and which will constitute the essence of his eternal happiness?

She says that the Beatific Vision of God is the highest form of divine knowledge possible to angels or to men. It is a supreme participation in the very knowledge that God has of himself, in the very life of God. Here we think of St. Paul's explanation: "We see now through a glass in a dark manner, but then face-to-face. We know now, in part, but then we shall know even as we are known.[271]

On earth we can know God in many ways. We can know him by faith, for example; we can contact him by prayer; we can reach out to possess him by charity; we can reflect upon him in meditation; we can even behold him in a singular manner in contemplation; but none of these modes of knowledge can compare with that which we shall have in heaven. Here on earth all knowledge is transitory and incomplete; in heaven it will be permanent, perfect, and without defect, like an imperfect eye that is suddenly endowed with the light of perfect vision.

The Church teaches that what Man shall see in heaven will be God himself, not some sort of reflection of his glory, but rather a

[271]Cf. 1 Cor. 13:12.

face-to-face vision of him. Nothing in Man's nature could entitle him to this vision of God; it is a pure gift of God's love.

A question that naturally comes to mind now would be: Will there be any other joys in heaven, more akin to those with which we are familiar here on earth? The church answers yes, for Jesus himself frequently intimated this in his parables and other teachings. In His teaching on eternal life, he clearly implied that part of the happiness of heaven will consist in the delight of the senses now made perfect in glory. The imagery he used, moreover, to convey the nature of eternal happiness was frequently that of sense delight. St. Paul also alluded to sense imagery when describing the joys of eternal life, which he had beheld in vision. He said: "Eye has not seen nor ear heard, neither has it entered into the heart of Man what things God has prepared for those who love him."[272] Perhaps it was the remembrance of that glorious vision that caused him to exclaim on another occasion that "the sufferings of this life are not worthy to be compared with the glory to come that shall be revealed in us."[273]

Can we form any idea of the nature of these joys? Perhaps in this matter the glories of this visible universe may offer a clue, for as St. Paul also said: "The invisible things of God from the creation of the world are clearly seen, being understood by the things that are made, his eternal power also, and divinity."[274]

In this mortal life there are joys that come from the deeply satisfying beauties of nature — for example, the glory of the starlit firmament, or the vast expanse of the blue heavens by day, overspread with clouds of shining light. Then there is the exquisite

[272] 1 Cor. 2:9.
[273] Rom. 8:18.
[274] Rom. 1:20.

beauty of the ever-changing landscape, the vast expanse of sea, the refreshing breeze, and the song of the birds. In the social order, there are all the joys of home life and the sweet associations of friendship that make life so dear. Yet these natural joys are only faint reflections of the plenitude of happiness that Man shall possess in eternal life.

The apostle John, for example, was granted various visions of the social aspect of eternal life, if we may speak thus, in which he beheld the angels and the blessed jointly participating in the majestic ritual of divine worship. Thus he saw the four mysterious living creatures chanting an eternal *Sanctus* to the glory of God, and the twenty-four ancients casting their golden crowns before his throne, while singing a hymn to God's glory for the creation he had made: "You are worthy, O Lord, our God, to receive glory and honor and power, because you have created all things, and for your will they were and have been created."[275]

He saw, too, the virgin choir that followed the Lamb upon Mount Sion and heard them sing a new song that no one else could sing. He saw a great multitude that no man could number, of all nations and tribes and peoples and tongues, standing before the throne of God, and in the sight of the Lamb, clothed with white robes and with palms in their hands, praising God for the mystery of salvation, while the angels, the ancients, and the four living creatures responded with a canticle of their own: "Benediction and glory and wisdom and thanksgiving, honor, and power, and strength to our God, forever and ever."[276]

Splendor followed upon splendor as he watched the majesty and circumstance with which the never-ending ritual of adoration and

---

[275] Apoc. 4:8-11 (RSV = Rev. 4:8-11).
[276] Apoc. 7:9-12 (RSV = Rev. 7:9-12).

praise was offered by the angels and the blessed to the triune God. And the pageant was crowned by the vision of the redeemed standing upon the crystal sea, with harps in their hands, singing a canticle of praise to God for the wonder of His works: "Great and wonderful are your works, Lord God almighty. Just and true are your ways, O King of ages. Who shall not fear you, O Lord, and magnify your name? For you only are holy. For all nations shall come and adore in your sight, because your judgments are manifest."[277]

These glorious visions reveal that the same order and harmony that prevail in the visible universe are to be found in an even greater degree in heaven. There the whole life of the blessed is immersed in the glory of God, and yet amid all this formal splendor, there is a sweet sense of home, for Jesus frequently spoke of eternal life as a wedding banquet wherein Man would sit down with God at the table of everlasting life, when the doors of time should be closed forever.[278] Perhaps this is the most beautiful symbol of heaven, for since the dawn of time, Man has looked upon a banquet celebrated in the company of his friends as the most perfect expression of earthly happiness.

Yet in this beautiful parable Jesus has also given one of the most mysterious insights into the nature of eternal life, for in the parable of the Wedding Feast, he showed that no one can enter heaven without the wedding garment of grace; and it is likewise evident that of all the multitude of the redeemed who are in heaven, not one has entered by chance, but each is known personally to God, and each has been assigned his predestined place therein by God, just as each star in the firmament is appointed its specific location in space.

[277] Apoc. 15:3-4 (RSV = Rev. 14:3-4).
[278] Cf. Matt. 22:1-14.

In this parable, furthermore, we touch indirectly upon the question of inequality of merit in heaven. We know from the Gospels that God will reward each soul according to its deeds,[279] yet while each must have the festive garment of grace, all shall not be alike, for all shall not have merited an equal reward. We could express it in another way by saying that since all are not equal in merit, they differ in the degree of glory they possess.

Now we may ask: will this inequality in glory be a cause of envy or sadness among the blessed? The Church answers no, for to begin with, every soul wears the wedding garment it has woven itself, from its life's merits, and as he has woven it, so shall it be. Besides, however simple this robe of grace may be, it will nevertheless be beautiful, radiant with the light of glory. There will be no cause for envy, moreover, for every soul will be brimful of the love and happiness of God according to its capacity, like a large and a small drinking vessel, which may both be filled to the brim, yet differ greatly in the amount of water they can hold.

Thus it will be in heaven. Each soul will love and be loved in turn by God, in a unique and personal manner, and it will be loved by the saints and angels, too. It will be given its place in the divine household of heaven by God himself, and this place no one can take from it.[280]

The difference among the blessed, moreover, will cause neither contention nor conflict, for the glory of one will be the glory of all. Just as the light of the sun falling upon the earth enlightens it with its splendor, so the glory of each individual soul will shed its radiance upon the whole household of God. The glory of the greater will in no way eclipse that of the lesser, for as in the natural

[279]Matt. 16:27; 20.
[280]Cf. John 16:22.

firmament, star differs from star in glory, so shall it be in heaven. In this material universe, it is precisely the difference in light and magnitude that makes the beautiful pattern of the heavens. Thus, both the small and the great stars, arranged according to a divinely appointed order, equally contribute to the glory of the heavens.

Or again, we can consider the beauty of the field flowers in the spring. It is the variety of size and color that makes the exquisite pattern of beauty that is nature's fairest adornment. So it shall be in heaven. The glory of the greater saints will in no way impoverish that of the lesser; rather, it will enhance and compliment it, and in the Divine Household, God will be all in all, at once the adornment, beatitude, and delight of the Blessed.

In heaven no shadow of sorrow will ever come, nor will the sinister form of evil in any aspect enter to destroy the happiness of the feast, for we know from divine revelation that in the home of eternal life, God "shall wipe away all tears from their eyes; and death shall be no more, nor mourning nor crying, nor sorrow shall be anymore, for the former things are passed away."[281] In the supernatural order, it will be the mystery of the dying seed come true. For just as the seed falling into the ground dies, that it may spring up in newness of life, so Man likewise, after having undergone the penalty of death, will at the time pre-ordained by God spring up in the newness of immortal life, in the glory of the resurrection.

The apostle John was shown a vision of the Church in this its final destiny, beneath the symbol of the celestial city of the New Jerusalem, which he described as follows:

> I, John, saw the Holy City, the New Jerusalem coming down out of heaven from God, prepared as a bride adorned

---

[281] Apoc. 21:4 (RSV = Rev. 21:4).

for her husband. And I heard a great voice from the throne saying: "Behold the dwelling of God with men; and he shall dwell with them, and they shall be his people, and God himself with them shall be their God." And he that sat on the throne said: "Behold I make all things new. It is done. I am Alpha and Omega, the Beginning and the End."

And he took me up in spirit to a great and high mountain; and he showed me the Holy City Jerusalem coming down out of heaven from God, having the glory of God, and the light thereof was like to a precious stone as to the jasper stone, clear as crystal. And it had a wall great and high, having twelve gates, and in the gates twelve angels. And names written thereon, which are the names of the twelve tribes of the children of Israel. On the east, three gates and on the north three gates, on the south three gates, and on the west three gates.

And the wall of the city had twelve foundations; and in them the names of the Twelve Apostles of the Lamb. And the building of the wall thereof was of jasper stone, but the city itself pure gold, like to clear glass. And the foundations of the wall of the city were adorned with all manner of precious stones. The first foundation was jasper, the second sapphire, the third chalcedony, the fourth an emerald, the fifth sardonyx, the sixth sardius, the seventh chrysolite, the eighth beryl, the ninth a topaz, the tenth a chrysoprasus, the eleventh a jacinth, the twelfth an amethyst. And the twelve gates are twelve pearls, one to each. And every several gate was of one several pearl. And the street of the city was pure gold, as it were transparent glass.

And I saw no temple therein, for the Lord God almighty is the temple thereof, and the Lamb. And the city has no need of the sun nor of the moon to shine in it, for the glory of God has enlightened it, and the Lamb is the lamp thereof. And the nations shall walk in the light of it, and the kings of the earth shall bring their glory and honor into it. And the gates thereof shall not be shut by day, for there shall be no night there. And they shall bring the glory and honor of the nations into it. There shall not enter into it anything defiled; but they that are written in the book of life, of the Lamb.[282]

This is the home to which the gospel way of life leads us, the mystery of the Church in its final fruition, as it was revealed by God in the pages of the Sacred Scriptures, a city of light whose foundations are in time, but whose portals open on to the mystery of eternal life in the kingdom of heaven. Contemplating the mystery of this city, we can only exclaim with the Patriarch Jacob: "This is none other than the house of God and the gate of heaven."[283]

---

[282] Apoc. 21:2-27 (RSV = Rev. 21:2-27).
[283] Gen. 28:16-17.

Bibliography

Abbott, Walter M., et al. *Documents of Vatican II*. New York: America Press, 1966.

Aquinas, St. Thomas. *Summa Theologica*. Translated by the Fathers of the English Dominican Province. New York: Benziger Brothers Inc., 1947.

Breviary of the Order of Preachers. Dublin: St. Savior's, 1967.

Carlen, Claudia, I.H.M. *The Papal Encyclicals, 1939-1958*. McGrath Publishing Co., n.p., 1981.

Catechism Notes. Dublin: The Anthonian Press, 1960.

Catholic Encyclopedia, vols. 2 and 3. New York: The Encyclopedia Press, 1913.

Catholic Encyclopedia for School and Home. Vols. 1-11. New York: McGraw-Hill Co., 1965.

Daniel-Rops, Henri. *Jesus and His Times*. New York: E. P. Dutton and Co. Inc., 1956.

Deck, Rev. B. M. *Baltimore Catechism*, no. 3. Buffalo, New York: Ranch and Stoecki Printing Co. Inc., 1933.

Dempsey, Martin. *John Baptist de La Salle*. Milwaukee: Bruce Publishing Co., 1940.

Documents on the Liturgy, 1963-1979. Collegeville, Minnesota: The Liturgical Press, 1982.

Farrell, Rev. Walter, O.P., et al. *Theology for the Layman* (a series of forty-seven pamphlets on the *Summa Theologica* of St. Thomas

Aquinas for laypeople, published by the Dominican Fathers of St. Joseph's Province, USA). New York: National Headquarters of the Holy Name Society, 1941-1952.

Fortman, E. J. *Everlasting Life After Death*. New York: Alba House, 1976.

Healy, John. Life and Writings of St. Patrick. Dublin: M. H. Gill and Son, 1907.

Liturgy of the Hours. New York: Catholic Book Publishing Co., 1976.

L'Osservatore Romano, English edition (April 21, 1981).

Odell, M. E. *Preparing the Way*. New York: Hawthorn Books Inc., 1963.

Orchard, Dom Bernard, et al. *Catholic Commentary on Holy Scripture*. New York: Thomas Nelson and Sons, 1953.

Orchard, Dom Bernard, et al. *New Catholic Commentary on Holy Scripture*. New York: Thomas Nelson and Sons, 1969.

Proper Offices of the Order of Preachers, English translation. Washington D.C.: Priory of the Immaculate Conception, 1991.

Ricciotti, Giuseppe. *The History of Israel*. Vols. 1 and 2. Translated by Clement Delia Penta, O.P. and Richard T. A. Murphy, O.P. Milwaukee: Bruce Publishing Co., 1955.

Weaver, Kenneth, and James P. Blair. "The Incredible Universe." *National Geographic* CXLV-V (May 1974).

Sr. Rosena Marie

Sr. Rosena Marie was born in Ireland in 1925, the daughter of peasant farmers. Her parents emigrated to America shortly before World War II, and while waiting to join them, she studied and worked with the Irish Sisters of Charity. Aware of a religious vocation since she was five, when she settled in the United States in 1947, she immediately pursued cloistered life, entering a monastery the following year.

During her nearly sixty years in the monastery, she has taken part in common housekeeping chores, pursued sewing and embroidery, kept the monastery chronicles, led the sisters in song (a role called *chantress*), and written hymns for their collection of liturgical music, *The Summit Choirbook*, as well as for a private collection entitled *The Voice of Praise*. She has also written many articles and poems for Dominican publications.

But it is her study of Sacred Scripture that has been most important to her. She began this quite early in her religious life, but only much later did she begin to write the fruits of her studies in book form. In addition to several unpublished book-length manuscripts, she is the author of *The Gospel Way of Life*, published by Faith Publishing Company in 1994. She begs God to bless this new book, *The Mystery and Destiny of the Church*, and to use it for his glory.

Sophia Institute Press®

Sophia Institute® is a nonprofit institution that seeks to restore man's knowledge of eternal truth, including man's knowledge of his own nature, his relation to other persons, and his relation to God. Sophia Institute Press® serves this end in numerous ways: it publishes translations of foreign works to make them accessible for the first time to English-speaking readers; it brings out-of-print books back into print; and it publishes important new books that fulfill the ideals of Sophia Institute®. These books afford readers a rich source of the enduring wisdom of mankind.

Sophia Institute Press® makes these high-quality books available to the general public by using advanced technology and by soliciting donations to subsidize its general publishing costs. Your generosity can help Sophia Institute Press® to provide the public with editions of works containing the enduring wisdom of the ages. Please send your tax-deductible contribution to the address below. We welcome your questions, comments, and suggestions.

For your free catalog, call:
Toll-free: 1-800-888-9344

Sophia Institute Press®
Box 5284
Manchester, NH 03108
www.sophiainstitute.com